'Richard C Fulcher's prose sparkles like dew on summer corn and makes one laugh with wonder as you would at the sight of a new-born foal.'
Julian Barratt

'I would give Rich Fulcher a quote for anything. If Rich begins a career as a grave robber I will happily provide an endorsement, e.g. "Rich plunders the dead with dignity – he cad-ave-r hit on his hands." That's how deeply I admire this peculiar man's comedy.'
Russell Brand

'I have long admired Rich Fulcher. The deterioration he has suffered through the ageing process merely accentuates his madness, creativity and continuous hilarity.'
Omid Djalili

'Reading this book was like having sex with a tiger.'
Noel Fielding

'Funny funny funny funny funny funny funny funny funny funny and a bit sad.'
Danny Wallace

AUTHOR BIOGRAPHY

Like most comedians, Rich Fulcher is a former lawyer and Marmite Inspector. He has appeared in all three series of *The Mighty Boosh* as assorted characters such as Bob Fossil, The Ape of Death, and Tommy 'Cheese' Nooka, to name a few. He also wrote and co-starred in the extremely dark and highly flammable BBC sketch show *Snuff Box*, with Matt Berry. Rich Fulcher's *Thriller* LP has sold an estimated 65 million copies.

TINY ACTS OF REBELLION

97 ALMOST-LEGAL WAYS TO STICK IT TO THE MAN

BY RICH FULCHER

MICHAEL O'MARA BOOKS LIMITED

First published in Great Britain in 2009 by
Michael O'Mara Books Limited
9 Lion Yard
Tremadoc Road
London SW4 7NQ

A CIP catalogue record for this book is available from the
British Library.

Papers used by Michael O'Mara Books Limited are natural,
recyclable products made from wood grown in sustainable
forests. The manufacturing processes conform to the environ-
mental regulations of the country of origin.

ISBN: 978-1-84317-415-8

1 2 3 4 5 6 7 8 9 10

www.mombooks.com
www.richfulcher.com

Printed and bound in Great Britain by Clays Ltd, St Ives plc

CONTENTS

CONTENTS CONT...

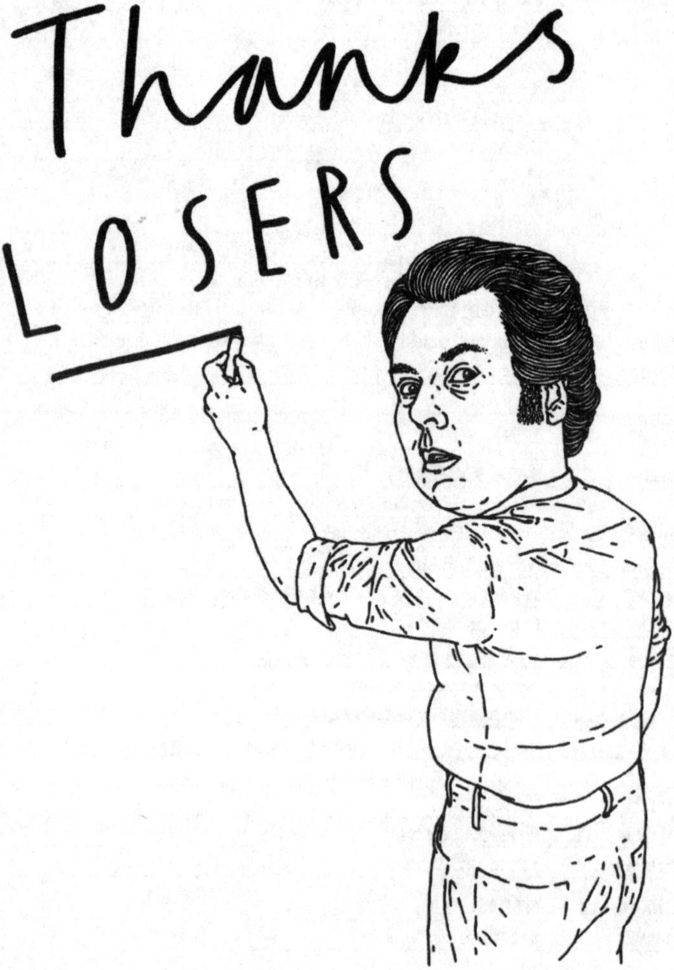
Thanks
LOSERS

ACKNOWLEDGEMENTS

As a first-time author, I naturally thought that books were made of steel and shaving oils. But not only is this not the case (it is actually a combination of lithium and steamed vitamins), but also I realized that writing a book requires a lot of help.

I would like to thank the following people who chipped in with suggestions and ideas: Julian Barratt, Robert Click, Shulie Cowen, Mary Pat Farrell, Dave Gassman, Amanda Holmes, Sarah Horton, Laura Krafft, Laurence Monji, Eric Stonestreet, Danny Wallace, and that guy from the bookstore in Westwood who kept touching my hair.

Much appreciation to Paul Stevens and Cathy King at ICM.

Thanks to the beautiful Georgie Blackwell for looking at drafts and liking them even when they were shit (actually, that was no help at all).

Special thanks goes out to my manager Glynis Hall, who has the patience of a Zen Master, and her tireless staff: Michael, Zoe, Bradley, Caroline, Michael, SJ, and especially Katie Kauders, who not only managed to help fine-tune while planning for her wedding, but she also helped wean me off my addiction to Tipp-Ex.

And mucho gratitude to Johanna Stein, whose editing expertise, constant prodding and maniacal devotion to eating bok choi made it possible to write and levitate at the same time.

Special thanks goes out to graphic designer Dave Brown and illustrator Mr Bingo. No two finer, funnier chaps exist who can work like rabid dogs, churn out creative magic and inhale copious pints of beer all at the same time. You guys are the bestest.

And a special special thanks to the editors at Michael O'Mara, Hannah Knowles and Lindsay 'Not To Be a Nag...' Davies. Without Lindsay's support and unwavering dedication, this book could not have been weaved.

Finally, thanks to my parents, who unwittingly pushed me towards rebellion whether they knew it or not.

INTRODUCTION

At the time of this writing... or the time that I wrote the book... or when the book that had been written by itself emerged out of the flames of Beelzebub City, the social phenomenon Twitter had just started taking off. Everybody say *'Tweet'*. In fact, when the disputed results of the Iranian election of 2009 roused the citizenry of that country into open rebellion, many people cited Twitter as an integral means of keeping the populace informed of the dynamic and rapidly changing situation.*

Ironically, while residents of Tehran were tweeting: *'Forces are tear-gassing all protestors in the town square, evacuate immediately!'* I was informing everyone, *'I just burned my mouth on a bacon sandwich'* and *'Don't you think cats are more evil than fish?'* and *'Wee wee wum wum ho hoo plops!'* It seems almost pitiful by comparison, but it was at that moment that I came to the realization that everybody protests on different levels. I mean, let's be realsies, not many of us have been in a situation where we are fighting for our lives to topple governments; no siree Fred. In fact, most of us haven't even broken the law (aside from the ones regarding the licking of non-poisonous amphibians – these laws are broken flagrantly and frequently). So what about us law-abiding people?

Tiny Acts of Rebellion (TAR) is written for us: people who have an inherent need to rebel... in little tiny ways. Not *'big acts'*, like throwing a lawn dart into a parking attendant's skull, but teeny deeds, like filling out a Congestion Charge form in Pig Latin. Not a *'big deal'*, like halting the entire tube system with stink bombs in protest at the high fares, but a lil' exploit, like farting at a friend's party and scampering away.

These acts should not be considered meaningless. If we don't commit tiny acts of rebellion on a daily basis, it is inevitable

* See the news.

that we would go on wild sprees robbing off-licences, burning neighbour's lawns and eventually swearing, just like Michael Douglas's character in that movie, *Falling Down*.

This book is a primer, if you will, on things you can do in your daily life to rebel (ebler if you're dyslexic). Each act contains a description (sometimes an illustration) of what to do. Some people may try and commit them all as quickly as possible; others may tell me to fuck off and leave them alone. Either way, you can do as little or as much as you want. There is a key to the level of difficulty of each act on page 12.

Finally, if you are actively keeping track of your progress, there is a box at the bottom of each act in which you can tick either '*I DID IT!*' or '*I'M LAME*'. I urge readers to take the book with you wherever you go. You never know when the motivation to rebel will come. Personally, my inspiration to write the book came at the Petrol Palace off the A149 west near Holkham, exit 13A, Gents... fourth stall down from the sink with the Greenpeace sticker.

I hope that this opus will be an inspiration to all who are aware that we are a rebellious people who want to fuck shit up, but at the same time we also want a fluffy pillow, a good Wi-fi connection and non-prison food for lunch. So enjoy the book, Happy Rebelling, and remember...

'There are no tiny actors, only tiny acts.'
Rich Fulcher, 2009

1 finger:
Delightfully disobedient

2 fingers:
Mildly mischievous

3 fingers:
Considerably chaotic

4 fingers:
Shit, are you really sure you want to do that?

NOTE

For the purposes of this book I will usually refer to a male, though the female form may be inferred. Except in cases where the tiny act makes reference to a penis, a vagina, or some delicious combination thereof.

CHAPTER 01

TRAVEL

CARS,
PLANES,
TRAINS,
POGO STICKS,
RICKSHAWS,
PIGGYBACKS...

ACT.01

DO NOT PERTURB

The name of the game with hotels these days is what I like to call 'cute honesty'. When the boutiquey Eastern European hotel clerk hands you a bill called 'The Damage', one is expected to laugh at the disarming sincerity of the statement. Ha ha, oh those charming Slovenian jerkoffs! Another example of hotels acting coy with fakey-fake bluntness is when they re-label the *'Do Not Disturb'* signs with something like *'Leave Me Alone'*. What next? Will they start calling the English breakfast buffet *'The Vomit Inducer'*? Should we expect to see a sign on the minibar reading *'The Money-Sucking Drink Cage'*? No. THIS MUST END NOW.

Here's a tiny act we can all do to strike back: make your own *'Do Not Disturb'* signs. This will require some arts and crafts skills, but you can handle it. Get a piece of cardboard (an old nuclear waste sign should do) and simply cut out the hole to doorknob specification and write any message you want. The more random the better. Some of my favourite signs are:

- *'My Asshole is Burning.'*
- *'I Hate Cupcakes.'*
- *'My Cat is Taking Some Fun Poops.'*
- *'Long Live Stalin!'*
- *'I am an Insane Nurse.'*
- *'Do Not Clean Up Blood.'*
- *'Who Cares What This Sign Says, You're Going to Fucking Knock Anyway!'*

That last one will require A0 paper.

I DID IT! ☐   I'M LAME! ☐

ACT.02

MORE FUN THAN A DOUBLE HIJACKING

How many times has this happened to you: you've just completed an eight-hour flight from Amsterdam to who-cares-where, the plane has landed and is taxiing to the gate, and you can't wait to get off the plane and shit out that tank of nitrous oxide you swallowed (for a friend), when suddenly the plane stops. Then the flight attendant announces over the intercom that you're going to be on the tarmac for a while and that you must *'wait until the seatbelt sign is turned off before you unbuckle your belt'*.

'*You're off your clock!*' I want to scream. Do you mean to tell me that if rabid elves were attacking the craft, we'd simply have to sit there and get nibbled? Screw that sound!

This tiny act will have the airlines under your complete control. While the plane is slowly making its way to the terminal after landing, unlatch your belt ever-so-quietly from its slot. (If you desire anonymous rebellion, simply cover the wickedly unbuckled belt with both hands so no one can see.) Keep in place until the plane docks.

There. You've done it. You've participated in a longstanding tradition of safety restraint rebellion which began with the untimely Seatbelt Massacre of 1876.

I DID IT! ☐   I'M LAME! ☐

ACT.03

THE LONELY
RED LIGHT

PHILOSOPHY 101: If you run a red light and no-one's around to see it, will you be ticketed by a falling tree?

It's late at night and you're driving to a hot-tub party at Jamiroquai's house. You're sitting at a four-way intersection at a red light. There's no-one around for miles. Your primal instinct tells you to step on the gas but society has turned you into an unthinking puppet waiting, waiting, waiting for the green.

Fifteen minutes later you arrive at the party only to engage in this exchange: *'What's that you say, Rihanna just left? You mean if I'd gotten here forty-two seconds earlier I would have seen her? She wanted to talk to me? She went home with my manager?! But he's seventy-one years old and has psoriasis on the entire left side of his body! Damn you, conformity!'*

It's times like these that we realize what kind of automatons we've become. Can't we think for ourselves? THIS IS TIME THAT WE'LL NEVER GET BACK, PEOPLE! I say, make sure the coast is clear and GO GO GO! These are forty-two seconds of your life that are gone forever. START LIVING! FEEL THE WIND IN YOUR HAIR, WHO KNOWS WHO MIGHT BE SOAKING IN THE HOT TUB PARTY DOWN THE ROAD?... I'M COMING RIHANNA... I'LL BE THERE, WAIT FOR ME, PLEASE... FOR THE LOVE OF YAHWEH!

Note: In this day and age of ubiquitous traffic cameras, this tiny act will probably only work in less progressive countries, like Romania, Tonga or Canada.

Note Note: Beware of the fact that this is a gateway crime and could lead to unprotected sex.

☐ I DID IT!　　☐ I'M LAME!

ACT.04
HEAD CHEESE FOR THE BORDER

It's inevitable. When I'm travelling internationally, it is virtually certain that I will freak out when arriving at passport control, even if I've got nothing to hide.

'Sir, how long are you staying in the UK?'

'Uh, a month, a year, I don't know, I'm a sex slave, stop talking to me, in the fifth grade I cheated off Kevin Ackle's maths test!'

Kinda like that. Exactly like that, in fact. I will admit to wrecking the *Titanic* if I stand there long enough.

The only way to wrest control from these demented autocrats is to actually smuggle an illicit item into the country. And if you're thinking what I'm thinking, the answer is, *'No, not just like that guy in* Midnight Express *who sweats from every orifice and gets caught with fifty bricks of hash.'*

You don't need to smuggle fifty bricks of hash. Don't be an assjerk. You only need forty bricks of hash. No wait, I mean you need to smuggle something that's only a little bit illegal, like fruit and pork and farm smells.

For example, just a take a small morsel of Cheddar in your make-up bag or a slice of ham in your trainers. Just enough so that you know you're breaking the rules but not too much that you can't blag your way out of it if you're caught. *'Ma'am, I kicked a pig and a piece of his skin fell into my shoe, then it got cured by the sun when I was hiking, and the next thing you know...'* You catch the nub of my drift.

I DID IT! ☐   I'M LAME! ☐

ACT.05

IS THIS SEAT TAKEN?

You're coming back from visiting your brother in rehab (addicted to pot, my ass!), and you're boarding the plane back to Wolverhampton.* The plane is half full. You realize that you've got an entire row to yourself. You pump your fist in the air, à la Norma Rae – not because you're eager to stretch out or create a fort out of those tiny pillows and blankies – no, because you've been given a gift... a chance to commit the ultimate tiny act.

You see, a seat assignment is a demand – an expectation of indentured servitude. Are you going to let a tiny piece of paper tell you what to do? This is exactly what The Man wants! Where will it end? Fluoridation of the water? Putting toenail clippings in fish tanks? Cancelling *The Wright Stuff*???

That's why it's incumbent upon you to sit in a different, non-assigned seat and wait for the shit to go down!

If the air waitress gives you a hard time, tell her that small-minded people will be the first casualties of the Airplane Seat Wars of 2012, sacrificed like modern-day mutineers and forced to walk the wing with tiny bags of peanuts strapped to their cheeks.

You may be *'seated'* in 5A, but if and when this plane goes down, your lifeless corpse will be strapped into 5C.

I know what you're thinking: *'How will they identify my body?'*

'Who gives a flying cunt?' I say! You'll be dead! They can use your corpse in a Latvian porno for all you should care.

Note: This also works in planetariums.

* Yes, Wolverhampton does have a 400-acre airport in South Staffordshire, so suck on that, anal pedants!

☐ I DID IT! ☐ I'M LAME!

ACT.06

M. NIGHT DRIVE-A-LOT

Let's face it. Once a person gets his driver's licence, it is virtually guaranteed that he will develop bad driving habits. Who will tell him when he is making driving mistakes? Naturally, you.

First, make a sign out of either cardboard or nonflammable wood.* Make sure it is legible to the other drivers on the road. Also, make sure the sign is handy. Place it on the passenger seat or if you have a passenger in your car ask them to hold it at the ready.

So, let's say you're driving and some old lady cuts you off, just flash a sign that says: *'You are too old to live.'* See, it not only instructs the other driver but also makes the roads safer for everyone. Another example: say you are just passing someone who's been going way too slow. Just as you are overtaking them, flash the sign: *'Any slower and you will have lapped the earth and gone in front of me.'*

Unlike the above, not all of these signs need to make sense. In fact some of them could simply warn motorists of non-driving-related things. Some useful examples are:

• Why don't we talk any more?

• My other car is a hotel room.

• I can't hear you.

• Do you know how to get to Willoubishervilleshire?

• My car has a crush on you.

• For sale (insert phone #). And then there's the car.

Note: Signs are far more effective than tooting your horn. Honking has lost its impact due to the fact that many people have been programmed, upon hearing a car horn, to stab the honking party in the neck.

*I won't explain the intricacies of how to construct a sign because I'm assuming you're not retarded.

ACT.07

HOTEL SCHMOTEL

This happens all too often. You're at a hotel and you get crappy room service, you slip in the tub, the maid enters while you're wanking... Need I go on? You're all set to write a long, scathing comment to go in the suggestion box when you have to check out and time runs away from you. And if you don't do it then and there, it will never happen, no matter how good your time management skills may be. Not even if you're as organized as Nigella Lawson on a cake binge. Never fear, the *TAR* comment card is here.

Simply follow the letter format opposite, fill in the blanks and you've got a quick, surefire way to get at least a few hotel staff fired.

Dear [name of hotel]

or should I call you [clever name change of the

hotel, e.g. Marriott renamed Marri-twat].

Words cannot express my [negative emotion]

at your [bad service].

Not only was [another complaint],

but [another] and [another]

but to top it off [last complaint].

I will never stay here again unless

[suggest free room] or [sexual service].

Otherwise, good riddance and may

a [type of animal] shit on your [body part].

Sincerely,

[fake name... just in case]

ACT.08

URINE AIR

At the time of writing, Ryanair president Michael O'Leary is considering charging passengers a fee to use the toilets on all Ryanair flights. It's bad enough you can't eat or drink without paying, now you can't piss without coughing up? Travellers, urinite! If this fee is enacted, we must have a plan of action.

1. Before the flight, pee into a container which you have brought on board (e.g. a small shampoo container).

2. Also, take a sealed plastic bag, the kind we are now required to use when transporting small liquids.

3. While on the flight, pour your urine (which is hopefully full of impurities or additives like blood or silver) into the bag.

4. Before you de-plane (hopefully after you've unlatched your seatbelt), leave the bag of urine in the seat pouch in front of you. If enough of us do this, it will send a message that urination is not to be shat on. It is a divine right, like breathing or eating pretzels.

Note: This becomes a four-finger act if you **a)** fill the bag with poo; or **b)** commit the act in your trousers and later shake it out onto the floor.

I DID IT! ☐   I'M LAME! ☐

ACT.09

QUEUE UP OR SHUT UP

You're about to leave your parking space when you notice another driver waiting for your spot. How do you react?

a) Leave as fast as you can in order to be polite.

b) Take the exact amount of time you need to exit the space safely, regardless of the needs of the waiting driver.

c) Hold your ground. If this guy wants your spot, it must be pretty good. Make him wait up to fifteen minutes.

d) Stay in your car until one of you dies.

Studies show that when a driver is aware that someone is waiting for his parking spot, it takes him 15% more time to leave than when no one is waiting.*

We must take notice of this innate rebellion and exploit it as a tiny act. Stay in that car and make them wait. Wait. Wait and then wait. Play your favourite song. Have a kip. Watch series three of *Torchwood*.

Note: This can be used in a human queue as well. When the person in front of you moves forward in an Argos queue or at a Westlife concert, don't move up to fill the gap, just stand there. Watch the frustration mount.

* I think there's a study, but then again I might have dreamed it. I can't really find it right now.

CHAPTER 02

FOOD AND DRINK

RESTAURANTS,
DINERS,
TACO STANDS,
WHALE
BLUBBER CAFÉS...

ACT.10

COPPER COINAGE CONDEMNATION

This tiny act is for all those waiters and people in the service industry who make snide comments *('What's wrong with raw pork?')*, forget orders *('I thought you said jacket tomato')*, and make your life a living hell *('Will your wife be needing a trough?')*.

If you experience any or all of the aforementioned scenarios, simply leave a tip of miniscule proportions of the copper variety. Why not leave nothing, you ask? Wouldn't that be the ultimate form of rebellion? Well, if you leave an empty table, chances are the waiter may think that you've simply experienced a brain fart and forgot, or that you're Scottish. No. To leave a small amount – and by that I mean copper coins – you are communicating to the server that you are on top of your game and have chosen to rebel against them with your government-backed *'bite me'* circle.

If you're lucky, you'll get some deluded waiter chasing after you with the query: *'Was there something wrong with the service?'* You simply turn around and say, *'Oh, I'm sorry,'* hand him another penny and say, *'There, that's better!'* Ah, these are the moments we live for.

This also works for bellhops, and large German masseuses with sandpaper hands whose idea of a happy ending is calling Fritz from security to escort you roughly out the door. This book is dedicated to you, Fritz.

I DID IT! ☐   I'M LAME! ☐

ACT. 11

DRINK DRUNK DRANK

You're at a business lunch talking about business. The waitress starts by taking drink orders. Your boss requests some sparkling mineral water; Larry, that dickhead from Accounts, asks for a Diet Sprite; Linda from Sales says she'll have a glass of tap water, *'thanks luv'*. The waitress comes to you. What will you order? *'I'll have a dirty martini, straight up, no olive, please.'*

What's the big deal? Just because your sober boss sets the stage you're supposed to follow suit? If this were the office Christmas party they'd all be snorting Guinness off the photocopier, but now just because it's a [air quotes] *'business lunch'* [end air quotes] we're supposed to drink super blue-green algae and pray? That's just not how it's done, people!

Six Stellas followed by a shot of tequila were good enough for our dads in the sixties and seventies. Sure, they had to get new livers, but the trains still ran on time!

It's not even crucial that you get shitfaced, although I don't really understand the logic of why you wouldn't. The key to this tiny act is to order alcohol in places where it is least expected. Here are some suggestions:

- A job interview.
- At church.
- During a medical exam or prior to surgery (offer your anesthesiologist a nip from your flask before he puts you under).
- When visiting your niece or nephew at kindergarten.
- During a swimming gala.

ACT.12
EAT IT AND WEEP

According to *National Geographic* Issue #235 (the one that featured 240 naked hippos), a third of the Earth's people eat with their hands, a third eat with a fork, a third eat with chopsticks and a third eat with taxidermied animal penises. This act is all about the first group.

First, make sure you're having a meal with some real snoots. Pick something up using your hands that you normally eat with a utensil and find a creative way to introduce that food to your gullet.

Many people have approached me and said, *'But Rich, isn't rebelling against good manners simply being a pig?'* (Actually, no one has said that to me because the book hasn't come out, but it's a great conversation to imagine, isn't it?) Hear me out, imaginary asshole. It's about freeing yourself from your strict mindset about social mores. Get over yourself. Pick up something and stick it in your piehole.

Some suggestions of items to eat improperly:

- Sculpt your scrambled eggs into '*La Pieta*', then eat with your fingers.

- Roll peas into your hand and pop them into your mouth like peanuts.

- Stick your fingers into tea or coffee, then suck the droplets off them. To add insult, offer your fingers to the person across from you.

· Eat food with the wrong end of the fork.

· Lick ice cream from an electric carving knife.

· Use a chopstick for mashed potatoes.

ACT.13
DIET POOPSIE

So, you're at your favourite fast food joint and the charming manwench behind the counter asks if you'd like *'a drink to go with your nuggety nuggets'*? Of course he tries to up-sell you the large 5-litre cup priced at £1.99. But wait a minute, maths whiz. If it's refillable, why not just purchase a child-size cup, sit immediately next to the drink dispenser, and just fill it over and over and over and over? Think of the freedom and wicked amounts of urination you'll achieve!

Similarly, many fast food joints and mini-marts hand you a lil' cup when you order a soft drink and then you fill it up yourself. Why not just give a fox some chicken gloves, huh? If they expect you to go back for more, then why, oh why, would you ever order a LARGE cup?

Many people argue that this does not qualify as an act of rebellion, but rather a penny-pinching self-serving act of indulgence, i.e. a desire for as much Mountain Dew that one can drink for 50p. I disagree with you more than life itself. Soft drink ingredients are cheaper than air so we're already paying too much. We're simply taking back what we justly deserve. We are literally sucking the life out of the soft drinks industry. SLURP ON THAT, DR. PEPPER!

Note: Do not commit this act before flying Ryanair.

I DID IT! ☐   I'M LAME! ☐

CHAPTER 03

ON THE HIGH STREET

SHOPS, CASHPOINTS, CHARITY MUGGERS, HOMELESS DOGS...

ACT.14
STEALING THE STYLO

a) Find a store that sells pens near the cash register and come up with an excuse to borrow one. Writing a cheque is the perfect ruse (except this form of payment is about as ancient as Madonna).

b) Try distracting the cashier by pretending that you've just thought of something like, *'Hey, can I get your number?'* or *'Oh shit, I've got to wash my robot tonight.'*

c) While the checker is scanning your items, casually stick the pen in your pocket or afro.

The beauty of this tiny act is that even if you get caught, it's such an honest mistake, who could accuse you of stealing? Who would do such a stupid thing? And if that does happen, just pay for it. What is the teenaged clerk with the Adam's apple acne going to do? Chase you down the street and restrain you with a tube of Clearasil?

> Justification: This act will guarantee pleasure and vindication for that time your weasel-lipped friend borrowed your favourite Uni-ball pen and disappeared from your life before giving it back. (Oh Uni-ball, how I miss you.)

I DID IT! ☐ I'M LAME! ☐

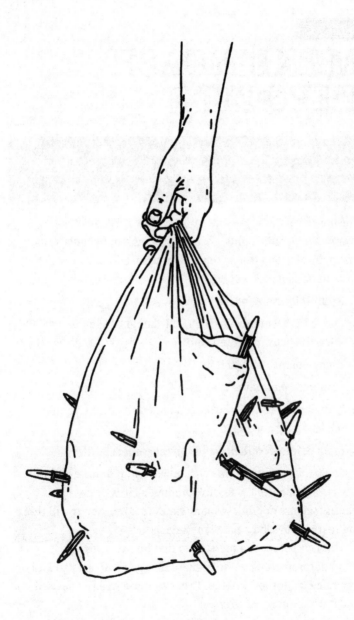

ACT.15

MAKE A CASH DEPO-ZIT

WARNING: If discussions of pustules, pimples, and oozing sebaceous glands makes you nauseous, then feel free to vomit on page 100–1. And then read on.

The big eye in the sky is watching you. Security cameras are everywhere. Traffic lights, changing rooms, public toilet seats, cashpoint stations. If they're going to be watching you, why not do something worth watching?

1. Approach cashpoint machine.
2. Punch in PIN number (which you should send to me at www.tinyactsofrebellion.com).
3. Complete cash transaction.
4. Locate most prominent ready-to-burst spot on face.
5. Utilizing the convex mirror as a target, aim directly into the lens and squeeze.
6. Extra points if contents lands on the camera itself.

If you do not approve of this type of behaviour or have such tiny, clean facial pores that you can't produce a zit, why not fake a realistic seizure or blink so many times that the viewer will think you're trying to send a coded message?

This tiny act sends a message to that fifty-two-year-old doughnut-munching security guard that you will not stand idly by while Big Brother watches. The revolution will be televised. And it will be covered with pus.

I DID IT! ☐   I'M LAME! ☐

ACT.16

WHICH WAY IS UP?

How many times have you asked someone for directions and been given bogus information: *'Uh, go down to the light, no, the house made of ice-cream, then right, I think... then... oh fuck.'* You end up in the red-light district in Vienna drinking absinthe with an ex-wizard – and you started out in Berlin!

Why not give back for all those times you've been directionally screwed? Go up to some people who clearly look lost and ask, *'May I help you?'* (see Tiny Act #23). Then deliberately give them the wrong information. If you are lucky they will ask you where a place is that you know is very nearby. Enjoy watching them wander aimlessly, looking for the Eiffel Tower when all the while it is looming behind them, like a giant French dick.

Variation: Wherever it is that they are looking for, insist that they don't want to go there. *'Oh, you don't want to go to the Eiffel Tower, it's overrated. Go to this place in Vienna instead. Do you like liquid hallucinogens?'*

NOT SO SUPERMARKET

I once went into a Tesco's to buy some semi-skimmed milk for my friend Blerge, and when I came out forty-five minutes later I had five cans of lentil soup, a box of frozen crabsticks, a plastic partridge, a jumbo pack of Walkers Crisps (rabbit flavour), and an extra-large bottle of blueberry-scented douche... But no milk.

If a supermarket were a town it'd be called Shitstorm City, in the County of Cock-eyed Cock. That's because supermarkets are pure, liquid chaos designed to confuse the shopper and deplete you of your money and time. What's good for the goose is good for the gander, I always say.

The next time you're at, say, Tesco (please note that I have nothing against Tesco, it is merely an example), why not:

• Move the prune boxes so that they're next to the toilet cleaners.

• Put the condoms next to the bananas.

• Replace the Flake Bars with raw chicken parts.

The possibilities are endless (use your fucking imagination). This act will cause the store's labour costs to skyrocket as they are forced to hire additional employees to re-stock and organize the shelves.

With a little work and a handful of friends committing this act on a bi-daily basis, you should be able to put a significant dent in the profits of, say, Tesco, ultimately resulting in the demise of, yes, Tesco grocery stores throughout the UK.*

Maybe, just maybe, the right person at the store will take notice and, as Michael Jackson once said, *'Make that change... Na na nah, na ah ah aaah... Oh shit, my nose just fell off.'***

*So take that, Sophie, cashier from the Tesco in Leytonstone, who turned me down when I asked you out to a Rick Astley concert. Bet you're sorry now! (P.S. My number's still the same. Call me.)

**What? Too soon?

ACT.18

YELLING! RANDOM! INAPPROPRIATE! SYPHILITIC SQUID!

Picture the scene: you're at some really smarmy dinner party and the conversation is stuffy and stilted. Just before Mitchell the host can tell you his latest spin on how Rooney should be traded to Liverpool, you yell out *'Faggot Ranch!'* The ice will break immediately and the rest of the night will result in *bons mots*, unexpressed desires, and silly poop jokes.

If you're not ready to attempt this act with friends or in familiar environments (that is, if you're chickenshit), you might want to start out in a public place where you can be more anonymous. During an important speech, why not yell out *'Party pants!'*, or *'Vagina!'* (pronounced with a hard 'g'), or *'I eat dogs!'* Please feel free to create your own, as personalized comments can result in a deeper, more meaningful experience.

Note: Obscenities always work. A short loud staccato-like *'Fuck!'* in the middle of a piano recital is always exhilarating.*

Other suggestions:

- While at a funeral yell out *'I like fudge!'* as you stand over the coffin.
- While in a crowded underground carriage, scream *'It's happening again!'*
- During a yoga class exclaim *'I killed Kennedy!'*

* When I was in college, I would often yell out *'Piece o' fish!'* at concerts, much to the confusion of others. I once whispered it to the President of the college when he shook my hand at graduation. He had a rather bad reaction because apparently he thought I said, *'You piece of shit.'* Oh well. I didn't plan on going to my reunion anyway.

I DID IT! ☐   I'M LAME! ☐

ACT.19

WOULD YOU BE MY SLAVE FOR FIVE MINUTES?

You know when you're having a skinny latte and mentally preparing for the impending descent of your testicles, and some dude asks if you could watch his laptop while he drops an ultra-large deuce? He asks so casually that you answer *'Sure'* without thinking, only to realize a moment later you've just formed an implicit contract with a grade-A wanker. Suppose an army of knife-wielding street urchins were to storm the place, snatch his computer and then run off: who'd get the blame? Oliver Twist and his adorable slumdog orphan gang? No, you would, because you didn't make a bomb out of Splenda and dental floss, rappel through the skylight and beat them senseless.

My point is, it's an unfair request for a stranger to make, particularly one that you're not sleeping with.

So this is what you do:

- Set yourself in an area where these *'Would-you-watch-my-stuff?'* requests are frequently made, for example launderettes, airport baggage queues, coffee shops, etc.
- Have the requester sign a pre-prepared written contract that states: *'In exchange for watching my............ [fill in the blank], I agree to provide the watcher the eternal rights to my soul.'*
- Place your face two inches from the object and don't move. When the requester returns, refuse to move until he pats you on the head, puts a fiver in your mouth and says *'Bless you'*.

- To heighten this act even further, ask every other person in the vicinity to watch the item with you.
- If it's a laptop you've been asked to watch, type something inflammatory like *'I ENJOY FISTING'* in 72-point font, and then leave.
- If you're lucky enough to be asked to watch someone's child for a few moments, you've hit the jackpot. Do you know what an Aryan child fetches on the black market these days?

ACT.20

JUST, JUST, JUST USE THE LOO M'DARLIN'

'A loo is a loo is a loo'
– Ancient Viking love song

Why do many establishments insist that the doo-doo and the wee-wee rooms are strictly reserved for paying customers? Don't you think that your bowels and lower intestine should dictate where you go, rather than some restaurant owner that hates cleaning up non-customer fecal matter? I don't know and I don't care.

What I do know is, you need to tiny act-i-vate this... I'm sure you've done it before. Just duck into a place that you know is off-limits to *'pee and run'*, *'urinate and skate'*, *'poop and schaloop'*. Make a beeline for the washroom and shut the door behind you. Do your thing (not forgetting to wash your hands – swine flu) and casually walk out. It's especially great if an employee runs after you with raised fists, like in the silent movies. What's the worst thing that can happen – you'll be barred? The barman jumps over the counter and cuts your ying yang off? You're arrested? Rules are meant to be broken, especially when duty calls (pardon the pun – unless you live in Chelmsford County, in which case puns are illegal and punishable by death).

I DID IT! ☐   I'M LAME! ☐

ACT.21

THE PRICE IS FUCKING WRONG

You're at a store buying some parsnips and your monthly supply of insect spray, and the checkout girl says, *'That will be £38 please.'* You give her £28 and see what she does. She says *'thank you'* and hands you your receipt. You bound out the door like a schoolkid in heat, spraying passers-by with insect repellent, howling giddily at their screams of *'For the love of Kilroy, stop!'* and *'I'm fucking blind'.*

I know what you're about to say. *'Rich, in these hard, hard, hard economic times you shouldn't be hurting the economy, you should be helping it.'* Okay smarty-knickers, I wasn't finished. If you'd have let me finish I was going to say that for every stupid checkout girl or boy that allows you to underpay, you must try to overpay the next. See how you come out of that.

And now I can see that I've thoroughly confused you. I'll try to type more slowly so that you'll understand.

You see, we live in a world where bankers have pension funds worth gazillions and can buy themselves islands made of semen. I know this has nothing to do with screwing over a lowly checkout person with psoriasis, but can't we all get together on this, people? We are getting royally pronged!! And if we can't all get a piece of spunk pie, I say it's time to fuck the whole thing up.

So all you checkout people, cashiers, ferris wheel operators, tellers, farmer's market attendants, publicans and, most importantly, pie saleswomen, be on guard. We will come at you with our wallets. Maybe not today, maybe not later today, but definitely much later in the day. Your ability to count properly is absolutely mandatory to preserving the economy. No pressure.

☐ I DID IT! ☐ I'M LAME!

ADVERTISE YOUR OWN PRODUCTS

Wouldn't you like to turn back the clock to when you were two, playing in the sandbox with Emma Gherkin? Or more germane to the book, to just before you bought those faulty products you never should have bought? Even with tons of information at our disposal, we still get schladonkered, bamboozled, and flagonzalized. It's time to rebel against misinformation and take the horny bull by the dick. Huh?

Here's what you do. Think of any product or service that you feel would benefit from a public advertisement, and then make that advertisement yourself.

'But Rich, I'm just a man who's starting to grow tits. How can I do this?' Simple. If your toaster is always getting stuck, tape a notice on the side that says just that: 'This toaster has a faulty trigger mechanism.' But don't stop there. Once the notice is up in your home, post a similar sign in the shop where you bought it.

What about your car? If you own a lemon, then proudly display your sentiments: 'This is the greatest Fiat ever, in the Land of Delusion!'

The more specific, the larger the font, the better for people to see. It's one thing to be on the internet, it's another to be out and about amongst the masses, trading information and learning about this thing we call earthworld.

Imagine if you saw a woman on the tube reading the latest Dan Brown novel with a sticker on it saying 'Terrible ending'... You pass a poster in the station of the latest Kevin Smith movie: *'Still hasn't made a good one since* Chasing Amy'... Then walk outside to a hot dog stand: *'Shut down by health inspectors last night.'* Imagine if you will... Oh, what a wonderful world this would be. Burp. Excuse me.

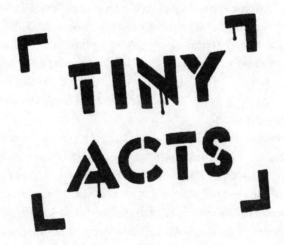

ACT.23

MAY I HELP YOU?

Walk into any retail store for a relaxing browse of Hawaiian shirts and gold-sequined flip-flop sandals and you're taking your emotional well-being into your hands. Because just as you're enjoying the feel of 300-thread-count cotton between your fingers, a store clerk will pop out from under the clothing rack to scream, *'May I help you?'*, causing you to jolt upright, back away, blurt out, *'Just looking,'* then run straight into a glass-paned door.

I don't know about you but it makes me anxious, like being cornered at a party by a guy who won't stop talking about where anthrax comes from.

The best defence is a good offence. Counter-attack. Thrust yourself into the store like a demented tramp and seek the sales people out. Approach them before they approach you. Kill or be killed. Once you've found them, and before they can even open their own mouths, use their own words against them: *'Excuse me, may I help you?'* See the confusion on their faces as you offer helpful ideas like, *'I think those slacks would look lovely on a heart-shaped face like yours.'*

Please keep in mind this may be dangerous, like awakening a sleepwalker. The subject may freak out and stab you with a hanger. *'No, uh, may I help you...? Does not compute...'* They may tear all of the designer suits off the racks and start screaming, *'I'm supposed to help you!'*, eventually falling into a shivering heap on the floor. But don't fret – it will be so funny you won't even notice the shop-clerk dripping saliva and 99p hair gel all over your shoes.

I DID IT! ☐ I'M LAME! ☐

ACT.24

ME AND ELEVEN ITEMS ARE AN ITEM

Your shopping trolley is full, you see an opening in the Ten-Item Express queue, yet you're not sure how many items you have. What do you do? Like most of us, you instinctively start counting your items and hope for the best. Nine (wasabi nuts)... Ten (goose spleen)... Eleven (barrister's eyes) – shite. Most of us would risk it, right?

Next time you're in the store, try deliberately to exceed the ten-item limit. Start with eleven tiny items. Are you willing to go higher? Twelve items? Thirteen? Are you man enough to add that peppermint-scented toilet roll and make it fourteen? Do I hear fifteen? Twenty-one? Will you go up to the female clerk with a toothpick and half a beard (she read my book), stare her right in the eye and say, *'Ring me up, bitch?'*

Imagine your exhilaration as you exit with twenty-two aubergines and a multi-coloured pen (which you stole, courtesy of Tiny Act #14) in your plastic bag. *'I am a rebel,'* you say to yourself, *'I am a rebel... Now, how the fuck do I get home?'*

CHAPTER 04

PARTIES

SOIREES,
WEDDINGS,
GET-TOGETHERS,
INTIMATE
GATHERINGS,
GAME NIGHTS,
ALL-OUT
PUNCHFESTS...

ACT.25

DVD-ICKWAD

This tiny act is aimed at rebelling against the societal pressure of being perfect.

Until very recently the majority of people would list public speaking as their number one fear. It has since been eclipsed by the act of picking a DVD to watch with others.

Here's the scenario: you're at the DVD store* because your girlfriend has asked you to select a movie to watch that evening. She has invited her co-workers over (including that guy who washes his pits with baking soda and owns five pet tarantulas).

Standing in the store you become anxious and sweaty as you mentally wrestle with 3,000 titles in your head, only to select something safe and predictable like *'The Sound of Music'* or *'Shrek'* an hour later.

This is a lose-lose situation where no one will be totally happy with your decision. Simply pick the naffest title you can possibly find and play it proudly. Although you will be roundly criticized for your choice, you can revel in DVDelight as *'Police Academy 27'*, *'Sorority Sluts 3: SPRING BREAK'* or *'The Passion of the Christ: The Out-Takes'* is playing, that you will never be asked to do this again. Ahhh, freedom.

*In the future, DVD stores will be replaced by the act of pirating movies on the internet. And even further down the road (five months or so) you'll be downloading movies onto a chip implanted in your scrotum.

I DID IT! ☐   I'M LAME! ☐

ACT.26

THE MEDICINE CABINET OF DR. CALIGARI

When at a party or get-together of an acquaintance, it is the rare person who does not snoop in a medicine cabinet out of curiosity. I submit to the jury, why not go one step further? Why not use or take something from said medicine cabinet? I've gotten some of my best cotton buds this way.

Find a toilet furthest away from the action and lock the door. Once you're in there's not much time. Douse yourself in perfume, take a prescription pill (if it's a Friday take five – why not – you've got a whole weekend ahead of you to recover), swipe some plasters, then get the fuck out. If you take too long to decide what to take/use, you should be prepared with an excuse: *'Sorry, I took so long, I had massive diarrhoea... five times!'*

Note: You may feel slightly dirty after committing this act but the feeling will subside when you realize that they will be doing the same thing at your next blowout.

Note Note: After this book is published, I will never be invited to a party again.

I DID IT! ☐   I'M LAME! ☐

ACT.27

GARDEN OF SEIZEN

You don't even have to be mad at your neighbour to do this – in fact, better if you're not. Simply throw stuff over the fence that does not belong there. This is especially good right after a party. Whilst cleaning up all the dishes and tinnies, if the neighbour is confused to find a chain of paper clips, a can of Lysol, and a wax ear in his garden, then you have won.

You get more points if you've been over to the neighbour's house and you throw identical items to things they already have at home, like that lavender air freshener they got in Morrisons or that really naff lighter with the topless woman in it. They will immediately think the partygoers got into their shit.

If your neighbour confronts you about this, simply look at them nonplussed (less plussed the better) and say, *'Hey, why would I throw that away? I need me some of that,'* and proceed to take the Lysol back. It's a win-win.

Note: This may prove difficult if you live on a farm or if your next-door neighbour is housebound and hasn't been outside since 1984.

I DID IT! ☐   I'M LAME! ☐

ACT.28
KARA-NOT-OKAY

There are actual Japanese businessmen who are, at this very moment, memorizing lyrics to songs, dressing up as Frank Sinatra, and going to the local Karaoke Club where they will silently critique your drunken rendition of *'Wild Thing'*.

This act is designed to rebel against these Japanese guys, and by Japanese guys, I also mean Polish, English, Slovakian, Yanks, Czech Rep, but never Swedish. It also works against anyone so self-righteous as to think there is a *'right'* way to have fun (see Tiny Act #29). I mean, we're not on *X Factor*, right?

When it's your turn to sing, botch the lyrics up mightily. Show them it doesn't matter. Life still goes on if you sing *'Wake me up, before you oh no'* instead of *'go go'*. Watch the guys in the back spew their pints of lard.

Examples:

- *'I'll never be your beast of Persia.'*
- *'Today is gonna be the day when we're gonna try and buy a ewe now.'*
- *'Gowns to the left of me, chokers to the right, here I am, stuck in the middle with shoes.'*

ACT.29
IT'S GAMEY IN HERE

If you like social occasions where you go to another person's flat and play games like Boggle or Charades or the ancient Hittite game of Smashy-Smash-Smash, then put this book down and slowly shoot yourself. However, if, like me, you are frustrated by rules, by people telling you what to do, and by the feeling of being pummeled once again into a senseless heap by an assortment of mindless frolics, merely because the hosts are socially retarded, then read on.

Tell a select group of people (preferably ones that enjoy Smashy-Smash-Smash) that you're hosting a *'Games Night'* in which you'll be playing, well, games. Right at the moment where you're about to break the seal on the Jenga kit, stop and say, *'Hey, you know what? I just decided that we should simply talk instead. Topic one: how inclement weather causes clinical depression.'*

Imagine the disappointment as Nick the solicitor from Newcastle and Martha the postal worker from Derby begin to weep uncontrollably. Ha Ha. That's what you get for wanting to be controlled. Suck on that Nick and Martha!*

Uh, sorry, that was too much.

*Martha and I used to date. Nick is still miffed about it, but between you and me, I think he's bi.

I DID IT! ☐   I'M LAME! ☐

ACT.30

NOW YOU SEE ME, NOW YOU (SLAM)

Why are we always expected to stick around to say bye-bye to the host of a party before we leave? I think it's just a way for the partygoer to try and get Brownie points by signaling to the host, *'Look at me, aren't I the best guest ever, thanking you for the party and letting you know that I haven't puked on your leather bed?'* Why can't you do all this the next day with a quick email or message by carrier pigeon?

In fact, saying goodbye can often take longer than the actual party itself.* So, next time you're at a gathering, why not tell everyone you're going out for a fag and simply leave without saying goodbye to anyone. This is known in some circles as *'pulling a Houdini'*. Feel the exhilaration. It's somewhat akin to being freed from a prison (albeit a prison with beer and snacks).

Once you've perfected the party technique, you can expand it to other situations:

- **Doctor's office:** If you find yourself wearing a paper gown, waiting for your doctor to return with six over-eager med school students in that room with all the tongue depressors... bolt.

- **Property showings:** Just as the estate agent is walking up the stairs to show you that fourth-floor flat, back out the front door you go.

- **School exams:** You may get a failing grade, but at least you live.

- **At the check-out in the grocery store:** Just as the clerk has rung you up and given you the tally, abandon your basket and run.

* Huh? Since saying goodbye takes place during the party, it is impossible for it to take longer than the party itself. Unless you're in a black hole.

ACT.31

'SOMETHING OLD, NEW, BORROWED & BLUE (MY BALLS)'

Aren't weddings wonderfun? You can get away with so many tiny acts of rebellion it's not even for real, bro! Chances are that the table at which you're seated (next to the bride's oldest brother who was kicked out of the Territorial Army for hypnotizing a banana) will have a disposable camera. These are designed to capture moments of you and other guests doing memorable things like smiling and hugging, mugging for the camera, and having your bananas hypnotized.

Isn't it enough that you bought a set of used bedsheets for fifty per cent off at Marks & Spencer, now you have to act as the happy couple's goddamned photographer? Why can't you just be left alone to enjoy some free top-shelf alcohol? And if it's not free, don't even get started! *'What's next, "my liege",'* you wail. *'You want me to hoover up the rice after we're finished?!'* Good Gad!

This is a perfect opportunity to eff some shiz up. First of all, find an empty table and swipe said disposable camera. (If you can't find an empty table, find the one where the groom's ancient third cousins are seated. They'll never notice you – and besides, the last time they took photos it was with a daguerrotype.) Then tell your date that you are now Annie Leibowitz. These people want memories? Start recording.

Some photo suggestions:

- Your bulbous, naked ass covered in cake (hint: even better if you can get a shot of it clenching the bridal bouquet).

- Random close-ups of things that have nothing to do with the wedding: a tight shot of an ear, a sheet of toilet paper, a garbage can, half a crisp on a plate. Some might call this a waste of a photo – I call it art.

- It's common knowledge that, next to an Englebert Humperdinck concert, weddings are the most likely place to find people having illicit sex. Find one of these awkward, alcohol-fuelled hook-ups – the kind that would never take place in any other environment, ever – and snap away. Extra points if one of the subjects is the bride or groom.

- If you can't find wedding guests in compromising situations, then create them. Ask the bride's blind Aunt Rosie for a kiss – then present your freshly shaved package to her face.

Believe me, when the bride and groom look back fondly through their wedding album, your diagonal shot of a urinal cake will be most appreciated.

A lifetime gift or a tiny act of rebellion – you make the call.

PRESENT AND UNACCOUNTED FOR

What greater social pressure is there than buying the perfect wedding or baby shower gift? It's too much I tell you, too much.*
Much like failing an exam (see Tiny Act #46), if you feel you can't quite cut the mustard and get the perfect gift, why not just focus your energies on fucking up big-time? Venture outside the norm of baby booties and twelve-slice toasters and his-and-hers Facebook accounts. Here are some suggestions for weddings:

- A giant fist.
- A wooden block that says '*bird brain*'.
- A hand-towel with a note that says, '*I'll get you the rest of the set if the marriage lasts.*'
- For her, matches, because he will stink up the toilet and for him, matches, so he can burn down the flat for insurance after she leaves him.
- A wire-tapping kit.

And here are some for a new baby:

- A '*My Baby Is A Future Burden on Society*' T-shirt.
- An Opus Dei baby leash, complete with first edition of *The Da Vinci Code.*
- A bib that says '*My Other Baby is a Volvo*'.

*It's still too much.

I DID IT! ☐   I'M LAME! ☐

ACT.33

SOUNDS LIKE A PARTY TO ME

You're at a super-loud house party where the only person you know is a girl you've just started dating. She's in a bedroom upstairs performing a sexual act with her ex-boyfriend. She calls it *'closure'*, I call it *'lemonade'* – because it's the perfect opportunity to commit a number of tiny acts.

The following are all *TAR*s that take advantage of the ambient sound.

- Put on a set of Mp3 headphones. Dance wildly and ask another partygoer if they've heard of this band. Hand them the headphones, making sure they see the dangling cord not plugged into anything. Dance off into space.

- Schmooze and mingle with other partygoers, speaking only in fake Eastern European gibberish or in Tagalog.

- Stand next to the speakers and mime-talk to people so they think they're deaf.

- When conversing, insert curse-words into your dialogue. *'Hey, great party, you dipshit! Really nice to meet you, you big ol' kiddy-fiddler!'*

After you're done, and your [air quotes] *'girlfriend'* [end air quotes] is still not finished with her *'closure'*, you can order a cab with her credit card.

I DID IT! ☐   I'M LAME! ☐

CHAPTER 05

HIGH DAYS AND HOLIDAYS

RELIGIOUS FESTIVALS, BIRTHDAYS, BAR MITZVAHS, MESSY DIVORCES...

ACT.34

CHRISTMAS TREE-SON

As a kid, didn't you laugh at the family next door who left their Christmas decorations out just a leeeetle bit too long? *'Hey, Old Man Murphy, the guy who collects his farts in old coffee cans, still has his Christmas tree out – and it's June!'*

But for every flatulent geezer, there are ten families (let's call them *'The Wankeys'*) who spend fifty quid on gilded ornaments in order to hang them on a tall majestic evergreen tree that they have displayed in their living rooms, and around which they will rejoice on 25 December. But as soon as morning breaks on Boxing Day, like a road-worn whore in stiletto heels, the tree is shown the door and left on the curb, where she will be picked up by a couple of sweaty trash collectors who will have their way with her and take her to god-knows-where.

It's time we became more like Old Man Murphy (coffee-can farts optional). Why the rush? Leave it up. See the expressions on your friends' faces when they ask, *'Why the fuck is your Christmas tree up in June?'* And then you smile and respond, *'Why do you beat your wife?'* Please note that this can apply to other holidays as well, like lighting chocolate Easter eggs on Guy Fawkes Night and/or to any other religions that decree the leaving up of shit for long periods of time (e.g. keeping your *Days of Thunder* poster displayed for two whole months beyond Scientology's customary 7-Day Cleansing Week).

I DID IT! ☐   I'M LAME! ☐

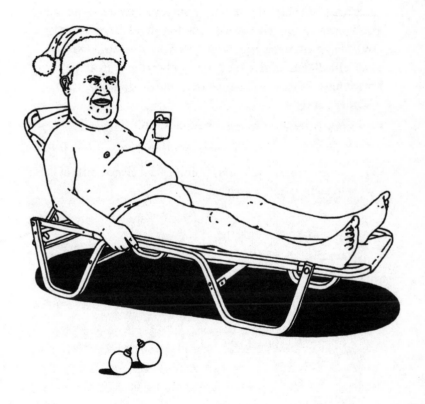

ACT.35

HAPPY MOTHER'S DAY, DAD!

I guarantee it will freak your family out if you are really nice and all gift-givey to your Dad on Mother's Day (or Mum on Father's Day). *'Why are you doing this? This is my &!$%# day! Give me my $&@!# iPod!'* You can give the correct person their gift at the last minute, before you're disowned and/or decapitated.

Other examples:

- Present someone with a cake at someone else's birthday.

- If you are at a pub for Dave's promotion, make a toast to Vicky.

- Go over to Claudia and Tom's for dinner and give a bottle of wine to their six-month-old baby.

I DID IT! ☐   I'M LAME! ☐

ACT.36

RECEIVE AND YE SHALL ASK

This act is quite controversial and I doubt that many of you readers will do it (see what I did there?). It requires a complete ban on gift-giving during the holiday season or any celebratory event like a wedding or a birthday. This is a lot of pressure and may require you to leave the country and change your identity until it all blows over.

Why is this a tiny act, you say? Gift-giving has become a racket – most especially during the Christmas holidays. The commercialized expectation creates added pressure and turns an otherwise nicey-nice thing – the giving and receiving of gifts – into an obligatory process.

I hate receiving presents when they are expected. It makes me want to eat an earthworm's vomit. There are two ways to handle this disgustingness:

1. **Give gifts when they are unexpected:** Christmas prezzies in July, wedding gifts during the divorce, Guy Fawkes explosions in May. The last one is more like a noise gift.

2. **Don't give gifts when they are expected – here's how:**

   • Go to your parents' house or any place you go to celebrate holidays or special events.

   • Don't bring any gifts.

   • Leave.

It's simple. However, be prepared to encounter hostility when people ask why they didn't get squat. You can handle this several ways: tell them the truth (how you bought this great book, etc); say that you're in a new religion that only allows you to receive (I know, it sounds sexual); or lastly, say you left everything in your car and need to go get it, then drive off and never come back. Easy peasy.

I DID IT! ☐   I'M LAME! ☐

ACT.37

SECRETING SANTA

How many of us have gone through the excruciating office ritual of the Secret Santa? You know how it works – you are assigned a person for whom you must buy a gift. Half the time you barely know the creep so you are forced to spend hours researching him/her, asking everybody *'What does Patty from Marketing like to do?'* in the hopes of trying to come up with a £5 gift that sums up that person to a tee.

Why bother? It's bad enough having to shop for people you do know. Here are some ways you can rebel against this hideous medieval ritual started by the Druids three years ago.

- Just give them the money. I've seen this done before and oddly, it's not usually well-received. I happen to think it's the best gift of all. The cash for a couple of beers vs. a Chinese butt plug? It's a no brainer in my book (and this is my book).

- Buy the cheapest, most random items you can find. Charity shoppes are a good bet. A smelly doll, an old chicken costume, a 2-for-1 coupon to see a Tourette's therapist.

- Give them office supplies, preferably from their own office. Or take a pen set from the boss's desk. It's sure to come back to haunt them sometime.

- Don't buy anything. Just give them anything you happen to have around the house. Some old pants, a burned pot, varicose vein removal kit... If the receiver gets angry and insists on finding out who gave them the bag of snake dandruff, plead ignorance and start looking for employment elsewhere.

ACT.38

HALLOWEEN (HULLO-WEENIE)

People love to be recognized. Case in point: me trying to get into a really trendy club:

Me: *'Don't you know who I am?'*

Large Man With Protruding Forehead: *'Please move along, sir, you're disrupting the other guests.'*

Me: *'But, but, but, but, but... Don't touch the hair, okay? I'm moving, please, not my magnificent hair!'*

Another time when people demand notice is at a Halloween or some other kind of dress-up party. People painstakingly spend hours upon hours to look exactly like Amy Winehouse or Gordon Ramsay or their favourite superhero, Billy Elliot. It means so much to them that you gush like a schoolgirl over the Megan Fox boob stuffings.

Why give them the satisfaction? What purpose does it serve to pat them on the back for looking like Hilary Duff? Get off your own duff. Be yourself, for Yoda's sake. Commit a tiny act that will drive these celebrity narcissists crazy.

Next costume or Halloween party, don't dress up, or even better, make the most minimal of efforts, i.e. just wear the Boy George hat; put on some sunglasses (it's so generic you could say you're anybody from Jack Nicholson to Stevie Wonder); or stay up all night and say you're one of the zombies from *Shaun of the Dead*. Then, when the costumed attention-seeker dressed as Noel Gallagher snarkily asks *'Who am I?'* just stare cluelessly and blurt, *'I've absolutely no idea'*.

Watch the steam rise from his tracheotomy hole as he desperately sings, 'And after a-a-a-all, you're my Wonderwall...'

'Nope, I just don't know.'

'Agghhhhh. Then observe as he ploughs violently through a sea of Ewoks towards Liam Gallagher, demanding his car keys.

I DID IT! ☐   I'M LAME! ☐

ACT.39

HAPPY BIRTHDAY TO NO ONE!

Did you know that if you randomly gather 100 people together, statistics dictate that two of them will have the same birthday? Try it. Next time you're queueing at a dance club, take a birthday poll and I'll bet my bloated bottom that you'll find two fellow birthdaters (and if you don't, then my bloated bottom is yours). That has very little to do with the next act – except that most restaurants offer little treats if you say it's your birthday. Sometimes it's a free dessert, other times it may even be a meal on the house.

Try this: next time you're at a restaurant and are on your way out, mention to the waiter that Ms-random-person or Mr-dick-at-your-table has a birthday and ask if they would do anything for them. Watch from a secret hiding spot where you can see the events unfold. If your *'friend'* vehemently denies that it's her birthday, sulks when the staff come out to sing a fast-paced *'Clappy Birthday'* and has the sparkler-laden apple pie sent back, then the birthday girl truly is a birthday dick. However, if she goes along with it and the table proceeds to sing *'Happy Birthday'*, then she is worthy of your Tiny Acts Seal* of Approval.

*Not to be confused with the singer Seal.

ACT. 40

MIS-GREETING CARDS

Store-bought greetings cards suck hard and make me want to slice the heads off a gargoyle salad. I mean, *'Best Wishes, Nephew'*, *'My Sincerest Condolences'*, *'Get Well Soon, My Darling'*... C'mon man! Okay, maybe your Nan would like this stuff but isn't she hopped up on antidepressants?

We would never *say* this manufactured drivel to another person, so why do we happily pay £8 for the privilege of communicating it in a card? Who are we giving them to, our most hated enemies? Can I ask any more questions? No?

I've lost count of how many times I've just bought any random card, crossed out whatever sentimental gobbledy-glook was there, and written *'Happy Birthday, Dipshit'*, or bought a kiddie card with a bear in a hat and simply added a zero to *'Happy 4th Birthday'*. If the card isn't really naff in its design, it's naff in its language.

Here's what you can do to rebel against the naffness.

1. Cut out a thick piece of paper to greeting-card dimensions.

2. Write a message on your card. Think of something you might like to receive. Here are some examples:

   • ANOTHER YEAR, HONKY.

   • YOU'RE SICK, CAN I HAVE YOUR SHIT IF YOU CROAK?

   • I'M SLEEPING WITH YOUR EX BUT WE'RE BREAKING UP SOON SO GET OVER IT.

3. Go to a greeting card shoppe (take the bus).

4. Pretend to be interested in the cards, and when no one is around, stick your card(s) in the appropriate slot.

....

5. Buy something in the store just to cover your anus. I suggest gum or a plastic rain bonnet.

6. Take a shower when you're home to destroy any incriminating evidence.

When a customer comes to the counter with a card that says, *'Happy First Shit, Son'*, maybe it will start to sink in with the manager that there's a new dawn approaching. The non-greeting card. Suck on that, Hallmark.

ACT.41

IT'S THE THOUGHTLESSNESS THAT COUNTS

We've all received thoughtless gifts – or, as I like to call them, *'social albatrosses'* (albatri?). What about the bobblehead doll won at skeetball in Blackpool? Or the brass rubbings from your dad's visit to Kafka's grave?

I believe that once you're given a gift it's yours to do with as you please. Well, not according to Aunt Carol, who won't stop asking, *'Where is the petrified taffy I gave to you from the House of Wax in Grimsby?'* And if you don't produce said gift, you're out of the will.

Some ways to rebel:

1. Re-gift. Let someone else experience the mini-hell of thoughtless gift receipt. See how your landlord enjoys opening the crocheted monkey tea cozy. If you are extremely ballsy, then...

2. Re-gift to the original gifter. Watch Aunt Carol's shock as she stares at her newly unwrapped petrified taffy, pondering whether **a)** you are the rudest person in the world or **b)** have early-onset Alzheimer's.

3. Return the gift to the store... in clear view of the giver. When you receive the cash refund, make a big show of kissing the bills before putting them in your pocket.

And finally, my favourite...

4. Destroy the gift on video, upload it to YouTube and forward the
link to the gifter. Do it in a creative way, such as:

  • Use a steamroller (note: make friends with someone who
    owns a steamroller).
  • Have a sixteen-stone man sit upon it.
  • Blow it up with a North Korean missile.

CHAPTER 06

BIG BROTHER

GOVERNMENT,
LAWS,
REGULATIONS,
DICTUM,
DO THIS OR ELSE...

ACT.42
PARK-OLEPSY

All right, I'm going to say it: parking enforcement is merely an insidious means by which cities crack down on, and suck more money away from, its powerless and generally law-abiding citizens. Who cares if there's a gang of hoodies hurling rocks at your crotch?! There are expired cars to fine! We all know there's no money in crime fighting, but hire a hundred parking attendants to molest the citizenry with countless fines – it's like striking oil in a barrel.

How do we rebel against such a relentless force? Well, we can't really. In the future, we will pay automatic fines for just fantasizing about automobiles. However, there is something we can do. If you see a car at a meter that is about to expire, put money in it. This is doubly sweet if you can do it right before the parking attendant is about to pounce on it. And it is triply sweet if the car is a brown 1987 Mazda with the licence plate EY53 RRX.

Remember, the less money the city makes on parking, the fewer flats our mayors can rent for those *Eyes Wide Shut* orgies and Masonic steak nights.

I DID IT! ☐   I'M LAME! ☐

ACT.43

DRINKEY NO DRIVEY

Technically, if you are pissed and in the driver's seat of a car, you can get nabbed for drink driving in the UK. Don't quote me on this (but do quote me that *'Gordon Brown has an anal fissure with a squirrel in it'*), but here's a fun way to rebel and you can do it in the confines of your own driveway/carpark.

Step 1. Get shitfaced out of your mind, you know, like you normally do.

Step 2. Get the keys to your car.

Step 3. Get in the car.

Step 4. Put the keys in the ignition.

Stop 5. Congratulations, you've done it. Now quick, get out!

P.S. Don't write me later saying, *'Rich, Rich, I did what you said then I drove into Wembley Arena in the middle of Iron Maiden Night and now I'm facing up to thirteen years hard labour in a Hungarian prison.'* Read the disclaimer on the back cover, dick-breath. You're on your own.

ACT.44
URINE THE MONEY

If you're a man (or a very masculine lady), chances are that you've already exercised this tiny act countless times. Don't act like you don't know what I'm talking about: going number one in the garden; sending your golden showers down the kitchen sink; draining your trouser snake into a Coke can during your third straight viewing of *The Deer Hunter*...

The key is to let it flow in a forbidden place – the more unexpected the better. No, this is not a mere prank, it is rebellion against the conventions of city planning and plumbing in general.

Many women have never ventured in this arena. For you lasses, this is truly rebellious. Why should you be expected to limit yourself to relieving your bladder where there happen to be indoor pipes? Think back to when we roamed the earth, before language, before culture... y'know, back in the eighties.

Get a little creative. Yes, doing it in the swimming pool qualifies as a tiny act and I have done this... A LOT. How about the side of your office building? A fountain? A trampoline? The opposite-sex toilet? A shot glass on the desk of your local council member?

Note: I will now never be invited to anyone's pool again.

I DID IT! ☐   I'M LAME! ☐

ACT.45

NEWSFLASH(ER)

You're going to an art museum with your nephew Damien, who has recently set fire to his primary school (apparently, it was an accident), and just as you enter, you spot a camera crew. Upon closer inspection, you realize that London mayor Boris Johnson is addressing the press about new arts funding for the city. What do you do? Walk past... Or tiny it up?

As he drones on, I suggest you get behind him and make your presence known. Yes, there are lots of yobbos who pogo up and down behind the camera and make general arsewipes of themselves just to be seen, but that's not what you're doing. You are committing a rebellious act by daring to make light of a semi-serious political office.

Be subtle. Pick your nose ever-so-delicately. Twiddle the bogey with your fingers – no sudden movements please – and flick it towards the cameras. Remember, heavy on the subtlety. You want to remain on camera until the media have finished filming. That way, they can't edit you out.

As you watch the news that evening with your nephew – who was recently arrested for knifing a Vermeer – you can feel proud that you have actively participated in the political process and cleaned out your nose at the same time.

I DID IT! ☐   I'M LAME! ☐

ACT.46
YOU'VE GOT FAIL

People, rebel against all those times you pulled an all-nighter smoking Silk Cuts, injecting caffeine and other stimulants into your crotch, and running on a treadmill, only to get a D minus on your final exam. Why not fail an exam deliberately, especially if you've got nothing to lose? If you even have the slightest inkling you can't pass, why not tank gloriously instead of try miserably? For example, if you're taking a driving test, why not sideswipe a traffic cone, use hand signals inside the car, give yourself a haircut... just don't be boring. People try to succeed but they rarely try to fail. Soak in the sweet smell of loserdom.

Taking an employment test for a shitty job you don't even want? Try taking the test so you spell out your name with the circled letters. Or pick a letter and go for it throughout (my vote is D). Fill it out in two minutes. They'll think you're Rain Man.

Facing a probation-mandated drug test, and don't have any extra urine on hand? Light up that bowl and stop worrying about it. Chances are the test will fuck up anyway. Life's too short, and so is this spliff.

NICK YOUR OWN STUFF

Have you ever wanted to commit theft in a perfectly legal way? Please say yes or I'll throw fruit at your mother.

This is very easy to do and works best in public. Place an item that you own in a very visible place (non-breathing objects work best). Stalk it. Grab it. Then run away as fast as you can.

The key to this is twofold:

1. You must look sneaky. I recommend wearing a trench coat and no underwear, or a rhinestone-studded burglar mask with black-'n'-white striped Hamburglar coveralls.

2. You must act sneaky. Approach the object on tip-toes, waggling your fingers in anticipatory delight and saying, '*Ahh, at last, a 1991 Betamax version of* Mannequin 2: On the Move *is now mine, all mine I tell you, all mine!!!*' Then cackle devilishly as you bolt out of the dentist's waiting room.

If you're having a hard time '*acting*', figure out a way to forget that you actually own the self-nicked item.

Some helpful means to forget are:

· **Time:** lend something to a friend then break into his house two years later to steal it back.

· **Drugs:** get really drunk, stoned or brain-addled so that the TV you are stealing is actually a giant toad full of glops for eyes.

· **Hypnotism:** Hire a hypnotist to convince you that the stuff you own is not yours and that nicking it would be the best thing ever. Please make sure they are a licensed hypnotist and not an alcoholic wizard.

If you do this properly, you may be stopped by a well-meaning citizen or a community cop with nothing better to do. If you are apprehended by legitimate police or armed vigilantes, you've won! Try and keep your dirty little secret until just before the beatings start. Ah, the beatings. How I miss them so.

CHAPTER 07

GENERAL MISCHIEF

HARMLESS LIES, FALSE REPRESENTATION, SECRET ACTIVITIES, OBSCENITIES...

ACT.48

ARE YOU READING FUCK YOU THIS?

We've all done the following: you're telling your boyfriend a story about how you thought you lost your cat but then you found it hiding under your mattress playing with a piece of string cheese, and you start to think your bf isn't listening. So you throw in an obvious lie or incredible statement, like *'Jeremy Clarkson dyes his pubes with lemon curd,'* to check if he is paying attention. Sure it's petty, and an indicator that you're a likely sociopath – but oh, how it works!

Why not use this tactic and get back at all those dull-eyed bureaucrats who simply nod their head without ever listening to a word you're saying?

So, you're telling the woman at the Job Centre about your work skills and you mention *'illegal gerbil fighting'* as one of them. Or you're arguing about your parking fine and in the middle of telling the attendant you couldn't have been parked longer than fifteen minutes, you casually slip in *'because I'm Zartron the Enabler, who has six elbows and can combust candy with his eyes'*.

This is a win-win situation because if the recipient of this statement ignores you, you have successfully rebelled against the Kafka-esque nature of bureaucracy. However, if the clerk responds, *'Excuse me?'*, then you have awakened him out of his stupor and may actually get some attention (even if it's in the form of negative attention like a door slammed in your face or a slap on the gonads).

Note: I have inserted one of these somewhere in the book. If you can spot it and send it to my website, you will get a free turkey go-fuck-yourself sandwich.

I DID IT! ☐   I'M LAME! ☐

ACT.49

DO YOU KNOW WHO I AM?

Okay, I'll admit it, I'm an E-List Celebrity so I get a shitload of pussy. But my awesome life is beside the point.* This is an act that demonstrates how stupid the whole VIP thing is.

Let me paint the scene: you're in a hip club queue waiting to get in (this is so foreign to me – ho ho hee hee ha ha ho! – forget what I said in Tiny Act #38), and the guy in front of you pulls out the ole *'Do you know who I am?'* card. Chances are, if he has to use it, it's not gonna fly.

So if the guy at the door turns him away, casually mention to the doorman as you're entering: *'Wow, I can't believe you turned down [made-up name]. He's fucking amazing.'* Feel free to embellish whatever you want but make sure it doesn't contradict the punter's story. *'Wow, you turned down Flip Soriasis. He was awesome in* Trainspotting.' Throw in a little fact amongst your group for good measure: *'Wasn't he married to Sade for a year?'* and then walk in and never speak of it again.

The doorman will be trying all night to figure out who that guy was and feeling bad about himself for turning him away. That's the irony. All it takes is a little notoriety and you've turned someone from nobody to somebody. And one day you're on a hit show, the next, you're selling your bodily fluids to a priest in Somerset. Uh, that's not me, that's uh... I've gotta go.

*At the time of writing, I am currently living in a treehouse made of computer boxes.

I DID IT! ☐ I'M LAME! ☐

ACT.50

HAROLD, LOOK IT'S AN OLD CHURCH!

Do you live in a city or town invaded by inbred Yank tourists (see Tiny Act #16)? If so, don't worry. There are acts one can do to stem the tide of creepy families invading places in your town that you never see yourself.

1. Offer to take a group picture. Make sure your thumb is blocking the photo. Alternatively, take a pic of the very tip of the cathedral but with no Uncle Jack in it.

2. Give them deliberately wrong info. *'See that statue, that's St. Buckton, the patron saint of colostomy.'* Even offer a small tour of made-up sights, one of which is your house – the former sleeping quarters of Robin Hood.

3. You know those horror movies where the new people in town are avoided by the townspeople? Go up to a group, beaming, and ask if they are tourists. When they say *'yes'*, immediately frown, turn the other direction and emit a scream of *'Head for the hills!'*

Hopefully, these tiny acts will force tourists to rethink their holiday plans and go to Björk's house instead.

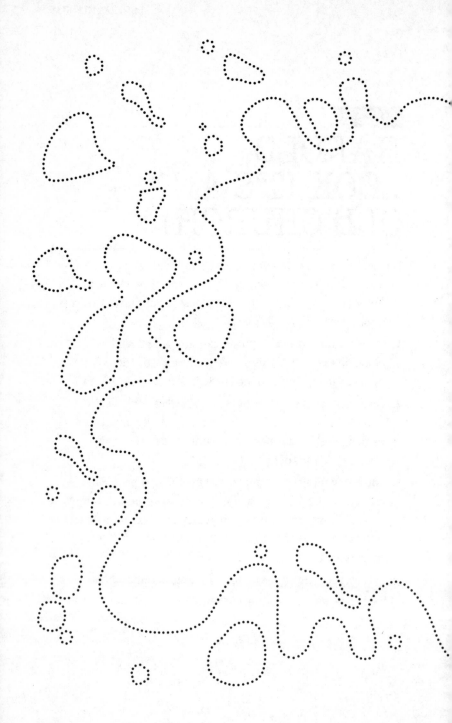

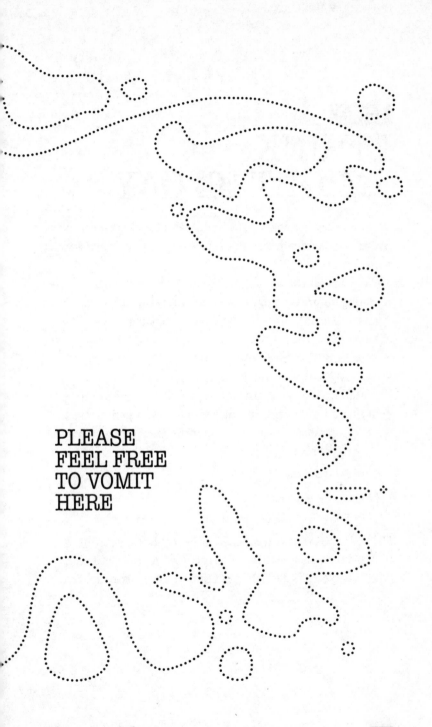

PLEASE
FEEL FREE
TO VOMIT
HERE

ACT.51

I THINK
I MIGHT BE GAY

We've all been in a conversation when a sudden loud noise like a train or a pneumatic drill or a squawking yellow-bellied warbler interrupts.

Why not take advantage of this situation and divulge some revealing information the second the noise abates? For example, you're talking to your mum about how you hate this one class at school:

'And the professor doesn't even take my question and then he – [TRAIN NOISE] ... [TRAIN NOISE STOPS] *– so I think I might be gay.'*

Naturally, you can't plan for these situations (unless you park yourself under a train trestle all day and invite friends to meet you), so you must be prepared. Some other possible revelations to have in your back pocket:

- *'My dad's a whore.'*
- *'I sexually harassed a Mini...'*
- *'... And that's how I killed a monkey.'*

FINAL THOUGHT: So in conclusion, I'm confident you will find this act to be – [SHOTGUN BLAST!] ... [CANNON BOOM!] ... [FIREWORKS FSSSSSHHHH!] – I've never touched myself.

I DID IT! ☐   I'M LAME! ☐

ACT.52

GOING DOWN

Picture this: the doors to the lift open and a woman is seen screaming, *'Get away from me! Your penis smells like burned popcorn!'* The next person entering the elevator will be flabbergasted to see that there is no one else there – hello, tiny act!

The trick is: well before the doors open, start talking as though someone else is with you, then... Boom! The moment the doors open, stop in mid-sentence and look as stone-faced as possible – allow no reaction whatsoever.

Also, make certain that you're not mistaken for being on your mobile. It helps if you are describing actions, like:

(Laughter) *'Stop tickling me... Stop it, stop it or I'll –'*

(Doors open, stranger gets in.)

Confusion ensues.

Hilarity is magnified 3.4 times if you are in a lift packed with strangers when initiating this act.

'What's the rebellion here, Rich? I've noticed that a lot of your acts are just silly pranks, and aren't rebelling against the status quo, as you claimed.'

Oh, shut up. You try writing a book, you questioning twat.

I never did like you.

You're a twat.

ACT.53

TO SLEEP, PERCHANCE TO SCREAM

Do you know that people often sleep in the same place every night? How fucked up is that? Who makes up these sleep rules? Why not mix it up a little? Don't let consistency hobgoblin your little mind!

The next time you're at a friend's flat to watch a game, pick a point in the evening at which to say, *'I'm sleeping over tonight.'* Then, when your slightly confused old college flatmate starts to pull out the hide-a-sofa, hold up your hand and say, *'No thanks, I'll take my sleep in the laundry basket.'*

Think how alive you'll feel at having broken the monotony.

Some examples of interesting places to sleep:

- Your car
- Office
- Cemetery
- Nuclear facility

OK, some of these sound like high-school dares, but what harm would it do for you to crash in your cat's litter tray one night?

Note: Sleeping in your bathtub while on hallucinogens does not count. That's simply called *'Tuesday'*.

I DID IT! ☐   I'M LAME! ☐

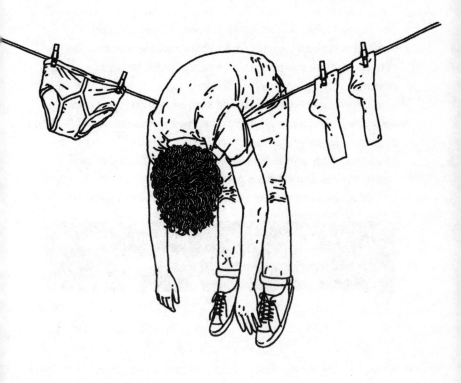

ACT.54

'ANNOUNCEMENT: THERE IS NO ANNOUNCEMENT'

There are so many announcements these days from stores, TV presenters, street preachers, flight attendants and dictators, it's enough to make an announcement about it. Ha! Or better yet, commit a tiny act by simply gathering a group of people to listen to your proclamation, then saying nothing. *'All right, people, can I get your attention, please? Gather round, that's right... You, in the blue, yes, you... Get off that tractor... Okay!'* Then walk away.

I know this seems like a waste of time and energy but it will result in confusion, which is good, n'est-ce pas? *'Did I just catch the tail end of something? Does he want us to follow him? He's really cute!'*

Variation: Whip the crowd you've gathered into a frenzy, getting them to chant, *'NO MORE ANNOUNCEMENTS, NO MORE ANNOUNCEMENTS!'*

I DID IT! ☐   I'M LAME! ☐

ACT.55

I NOW MISPRONOUNCE YOU...

Deliberately mispronouncing words is one of the best ways to tell if someone is a dick. It's a dick litmus test, otherwise known as a dickmus test. Try it with your friends and it may change the way you think about them. If, for example, you tell a friend that you're going to a Bon Jon Bovi concert and he bounces back with, *'It's Jon Bon Jovi, you flaming asswipe'*, then you may not want to make him your best man.

Here are some other suggestions and variations:

- At a restaurant, order something outrageously incorrectly. For example, pronounce penne pasta as *'pen paystay'*. This is especially good if it's a first date.

- Mispronounce the name of the city you're in and see what level of anger people reach when they correct you. *'It's Milton Keynes, not Keys!'*

- Consistently mispronounce a friend's name – or better yet, your own (see Tiny Act #62).

- *O-VER PRO-NOUNCE WORDS SO THAT EACH SYL-LA-BLE IS VE-RY DIS-TINCT.*

- Behave like a foreigner, speaking loudly and slowly as you explain: *'I am not from this county, I am from Essex.'*

ACT.56

'IF I COULD JUST HAVE A FEW DAYS OF YOUR TIME?'

You're eating dinner and watching Prince play tennis. Just as he's about to serve, the phone rings. You answer it, thinking it might be someone important... but it's just a crap telemarketer asking if he can talk to you about your duvet cleaner.

You could do a whole book just on this, it's so worthy of tiny acts. I recommend the following:

- Try to sell them something yourself. Be insistent.

- Ask open-ended questions that will get the telemarketer talking like: *'How does the Abdominizer work?'* or *'What's the candidate's stance on taxes?'* When the caller starts to answer, set down the phone and moan as if masturbating. Occasionally interrupt with *'Ohhh, yessy!'* and ask them to say *'melon fever'* over and over.

- Say to the telemarketer, *'Wait just a minute, let me get my pen.'* Then walk away for twenty minutes.

- Pretend there's an emergency. *'Are you the police? My eyes are on fire!'* Usually this will stop them.

- Every time the telemarketer asks a question, breathe heavily into the phone.

- Say, *'Chop, chop, chop into the slop, slop, slop.'* Repeat.

- Answer their questions only with lines taken from your favourite movie.

• Say you've got another call on hold and pretend to '*click*' over...
  Then start to cry and pretend that you're talking to someone
  from the suicide hotline.

You talkin' to me?
You talkin' to me?
Huh?
Then who the hell else
are you talking...
You talkin' to me?

☐ I DID IT! ☐ I'M LAME!

ACT.57
LIFE-JACK

You're on the tube whistling your favourite Ice-T song when, out of the blue, someone starts whistling the exact same thing. This is not a co-inky dink. It is a common phenomenon called *'song hijacking'*.

It may present itself as singing, humming, whistling or thigh-patting but chances are, someone is bound to subconsciously nick your song and spoil it for you. You are forced to stop your whistling, whereas meanwhile that person goes on with their life, oblivious to the long-term damage they've caused. Your whole day is ruined and it'll be years before you're able to sing *'Let's Get Retarded'* again.

My rule is: *'Do unto others before they do unto you.'* When you catch someone humming your tune, start chiming in even louder than they did. Make sure they are aware of how annoying they are. Fuck them up big-time.

But don't stop there. Why relegate this just to catchy melodies? Why not *'life-jack'*? Here are some ideas:

- Walk at the same pace as someone else, stride for stride. If they trip, follow suit.
- Repeat to someone else what they are saying on the phone or in a conversation. Works particularly well if they're using a language you don't speak.
- Find someone who is eating; eat whenever your victim takes a bite or a sip.

I DID IT! ☐   I'M LAME! ☐

ACT.58

LET'S FOCUS, PEOPLE!

Ever been part of a focus group in which you are asked to spend hours watching a film or sampling a product, then prodded for your reactions and opinions, all for the enormous fee of £50 and some stale chicken sandwiches? Well, I have, and it ain't pretty... Unless, of course, you tiny act it up.

Usually, there's a smiley-toothed bastard who asks leading questions like, *'That pineapple vodka – exactly how good does that taste?'* or *'On a scale of one to five, five being supremely delicious, how does the Mercedes DSL 869 ride?'* I always feel pressure to say something helpful, like *'Yes, I love this vodka so much I'd nurse my next six babies with it... And driving the Mercedes is so smooth it's like cumming on an elf.'*

I don't know why we feel a need to be nice to the bastard. I think it's a quid pro quo for the awful sandwiches. It's time to stop it, so here's what you can do: be as contradictory as possible so nobody knows what the *TAR* you're thinking. For example: *'I love the turnip crisps so much, yet I also hate them more than life itself.'* This will be sure to confound the executives behind the one-way glass, but more importantly, will hoodwink some of the other members into committing similar acts of doublespeak, like lemmings jumping off a cliff made of bap rolls.

Also, make sure to mention the provided snacks any chance you get. At the thirty-minute mark be sure to blurt out: *'We're getting sandwiches after this, aren't we?'* If the answer is not satisfactory, feel free to get a chant of *'WE WANT SANDWICHES!'* going until they acquiesce or until you are escorted out by Cadbury's security.

If you're lucky enough to be using the product in the focus group, e.g. skin-cream, then after rubbing a sample of it on the back of your hand, fake a seizure and scream, *'Fire ants! I'm being invaded by fire ants!'*

ACT.59

SPAMMER SPAMMER SPAMMER SPAMMER SPAMMER SPAMMER WONDERFUL SPAMMER SPAMMER SPAMMER SPAMMER
(sung to the tune of the 'Spam Song')

We all get emails from Nigerian bankers, penis extension sites and one-armed nuns from a pond in Sweden asking for our hand in marriage, but what do we do about it? Simply deleting these messages is not enough, people!

Here are some tiny acts of self-defence rebellion:

- Send a response back correcting all the spelling and grammatical errors.

- Send an extremely optimistic response that cuts off halfway through. Example:
  'Dear Mr. Ungawa. So excited to give you my bank details and receive some money! Here is all o...'

TINY ACTS

• Drone on and on without ever addressing the email:
  'I love it when I get money, so this email is right up my alley. Speaking of alleys, I lost a hairy armpit off my doll in an alley once and it took four hours to find it. I was a boneless lad of nine at the time, and my mother – who was a pimp for all the male whores in Bangkok – wasn't aware of my dolly fetish. It would have killed her to know, because as it turns out, my eldest brother Cosine was –'

This act is not without risk as you may get them to try even harder in which case you should either ignore them completely or –

ACT.60

THIS ISN'T EVEN REMOTELY FUNNY

It's a Tuesday afternoon and you've just eaten your fifth sausage roll... Your friends are all at this thing called 'work', your local is still shut down because of the barf-in-the-toaster accident and you're about to flip to the *Sex Inspectors* omnibus when all of a sudden it hits you – that remote control in your hand is the key to your next tiny act.

Do this:

1. Stand outside your neighbour's window. See if you can change the channels with your remote. If it works, go to Step 3.
2. Buy a universal remote that works, wankhead. Go to Step 1. Repeat as needed.
3. Test drive your remote on the road. Bring it to your local pub or TV palace. Don't flaunt it, just casually change the channels from a distance. If it works, you're in the money. Lay low for a while like that killer in *The Day of the Jackal*, for here is where the *'art'* comes into it. See, anyone can just fuck around with someone else's TV and piss them off. I know. I do it on a daily basis. But if you want to be a memorable tiny activist, you must pick your spots (not to be confused with *'picking your spots'* – nine out of ten Filipino dermatologists say you really should leave those alone).

So, go to the pub during a major televized event like the World Cup Finals (naturally, England won't be playing; let's just say it's Brazil vs. fill-in-the-blank). Wait for a particularly crucial time in the match and go for it.

Depending on the size of your ball sack, you can change the channel, mute it, or turn the set off altogether. After the screams have died down, and if you still have large stones, do it again.

Be careful not to be found out or seized by an angry mob. Just in case, you may want to have a friend waiting in a getaway car nearby.

ACT.61

HOW NOW BROWN BOX...

Remember when you were a young kid and a package would arrive at your house wrapped in brown paper, addressed to your older brother, and you would ask, *'What's that?'* Your bro would answer, *'Oh it's just my special zit cream,'* but then a few days later whilst snooping in his room you would find the box in the corner, opened, brimming with corduroy dildos.

Here is a fact: all that is nasty, dirty, sleazy and sneaky takes place within the confines of a brown wrapper. Horse porno doesn't come in magenta tissue paper, does it? Nunchuks aren't delivered in frilly doilies, are they? Handy dandy anthrax from *'Ye Olde Anthrax Shoppe'* does not come in royal purple packaging: you can BET YOUR SWEET DERRIERE THAT IT'S BROWN!

Try this act. Put some pebbles in a box – wrap it in brown paper and address it to an old friend or cherished enemy.* Then put on your frilly thinking cap or underwear. The idea is to hint at the potential contents, the disgusting-er the better. For example, in the return address field you could use:

- Bedwetters Incorporated
- Corpse Hair Weekly
- Anal-Plugs-R-Us

You might also try writing in large black type across the package itself:

- *'Contents Include Battle Plans for WWIII'*

- *'Warning: Radioactive Minge'*
- *'Includes 6–8 Ransomed Thumbs'*

Even a simple handwritten: *'Fisting for Fun and Profit – ask me how!'* can be effective.

* If you have none, simply plunk the brown-covered box in a public place, then leave (notice I didn't make any Al-Qaeda references. Look, I may be dumb, but I'm not bleeding brain juice).

MY NAME IS...
MY NAME IS...

You know those moments when strangers in public feel comfortable asking you point-blank for your name? Situations like getting a dinner reservation or being called on by the comedian at a standup club. I mean who cares if your name is Frances with an 'e' or your last name has an umlaut in it? This is a primo opportunity to be creative and make up a fake name destined to shock and awe everyone in the vicinity. It is name-telling with absolutely no consequences.

What does the comedian care if you call yourself *'Crumpky the Magician'*? Why should the hostess bat an eye if you say *'The Tits McGee family would like a table for four, preferably that red booth in the corner'*? It's not like you're giving your details for some kind of important document requiring your real name like a marriage licence, death certificate, or an International Star Registry certificate.

- Saying you are *'blank'* from *'blank'* is always fun. Try it. I am Dave from Sweden, or Ian from Stability Cottage. I am Ronald from Sucko.

- Another good option in this vein is volunteering your name when it has not been solicited. For example: *'Hi, I'm Nibbles, do you have the time?'*

- You might also consider adopting a fake name for the entirety of a social event. Imagine roaming around a party with the name *'Fancy Wonderchuck'*. Feel free to add an MD or Esq. to the end of it as well. Knock yourself out.

- Change the pronunciation of your name each time you talk to someone. *'It's Joanna... No, it's Jo-haunna... No, no: Jie-high-na...'* Get increasingly angry with the other person's utter inability to get it right.
- Give names to inanimate objects like your car: *'Here, Janice!'*

The possibilities are endless. Remember, the more strangers are involved the better. It takes an extra pair of stones to invent a name in front of someone you already know: *'Oh, sorry Mum, I thought you knew that I'd changed my name to Speedballs Pocketflaps. My bad.'*

ACT.63

HOLD
THE PHONE

You have something delicate to say to somebody (anything from *'I've fallen in love with someone else'* to *'Your breath smells like spoiled milk poured into an old tennis shoe'*) but you can't quite do it face to face. Why not have a fake conversation on the phone? Do it in another room but make sure your intended victim can hear you. *'Yeah, no, I've tried to tell him to stop playing his drums in the flat... No.'* Then watch as he enters, totally flummoxed after having accidentally overheard your call.

If you want to make your point hit home even more, have the conversation on a toy phone or random household object, something like a stapler or a large piece of salmon. When the other person sees you talking into a snowglobe of the Taj Mahal, hopefully they will come to understand you are not trying to embarrass them (though that would be a bonus), rather you are just trying to make a simple point.

Alternatively, try saying anything that comes into your head. *'Sheila has a wart on her left thigh... and she sounds like a Russian tractor in her sleep... and who can forget that I AM THE WALRUS...?'* [sees partner] *'Oh, hi, you all right?'*

If your partner or friend is not understanding of your actions, do what I always do in these awkward situations – point and shout, *'Hey look, SEBASTIAN COE!'* then head for the hills.

I DID IT! ☐ I'M LAME! ☐

CHAPTER 08

ARTS AND CULTURE

LITERATURE, TV, THEATRE, ART GALLERIES, CINEMA, DUSTY BOOKSHOPS...

ACT.64

ART FART

We're all aware of how pretentious art gallery patrons can be. Dressed in black with a Noel Fielding haircut, acting deliberately aloof and staring... always staring at the art. This act goes as follows: walk up to the art at a normal three-foot viewing distance, preferably in the midst of a large group, and simply turn around 360 degrees. If you do this act with confidence it will confuse others into thinking that they are missing out on some unique perspective or approach to art that their professors never told them about.

Some other things you can do to confuse them:

- Act surprised and shout, *'That's me!'*

- Turn your back to the art and get out a mirror to look at it over your shoulder. Then say, *'I see,'* as if you've just discovered the Da Vinci Code.

- Look at some art and tell your friend, *'That's where* Withnail and I *was filmed.'* This is especially good if it's an abstract painting.

- Look intently at a non-art object like a bench or the wall socket. The less demonstrative you are the better.

I DID IT! ☐   I'M LAME! ☐

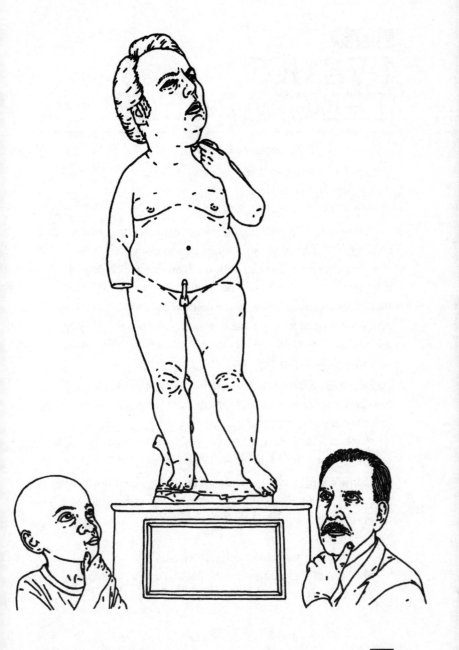

I'VE GOT THE CLAP CLAP

Who can forget this old nursery rhyme?

'Clap clap clap clappetty clap
Clap clap clappy clap clap.'
Inbred idiot, Wales, 1538

I really enjoy getting my clap on. When at an event, I always utilize the *'End Clap'* technique, i.e. I aim to be the last one clapping after everyone else (at least five seconds after is good). It doesn't matter what the event may be: the symphony, a poetry reading, a Green Day concert or a neighbourhood barfight. It puts people on edge to hear applause after they've stopped clapping. It leads them to think they've missed something.

Other claps to practise and employ:

Pop clap: The pop clap is much more ballsy than the end clap because it comes at an inappropriate time during the show/speech. It is short, loud and staccato-like. Best used during sensitive, otherwise quiet moments – like during a eulogy, or at any time during the *Vagina Monologues*.

The Slow Clap: This is typically used during a dramatic movie moment, like at the end of *Brubaker* or *Revenge of the Nerds*. However, the slow clap is best used after ordinary moments of banality like:

- You've just brushed your teeth (SLOW CLAP).
- You've just picked up test results that show your yeast infection is clearing up (SLOW CLAP).

· You've just had your parking validated (SLOW CLAP).
· Or immediately following orgasm (also works when you're having sex with someone).

The Seal Clap: When combined with boisterous grunts this is intended to sound like a seal... or a psycho... or a psychotic seal.*

*Again, not to be confused with the singer Seal.

ACT.66

PURSUIT OF
THE INANE

Most of us know things that we're not proud of. I'm talking detailed knowledge of how to get to Level 28 of *Dune*, or the number of *Friends* episodes where Joey said something stupid. Stuff that if you told your girlfriend it would require a lot of backstory like, *'I was trapped in the basement by my Fritzl-esque father and all they had were logic puzzles and that's why I feel the need to wank on them.'* (Even if that didn't happen, you need to tell her the backstory so you don't seem like a weirdo.)

Here's a way to fight fire with steam. Learn something entirely trivial or as I like to say, inane. Something that will surprise people. For example, if you are awful at maths, learn the quadratic formula and write it constantly on napkins in the office cafeteria. If you hate science fiction, then learn the titles of all the *Star Wars* movies, starting with the prequels. If you hate show tunes, start turning gay. It's a tiny thing, but it will cause a lot of people to think you're a freak of nature.

Note: If you can't think of anything to learn, just count the tiles on the floor a lot and check the stove.

I DID IT! ☐   I'M LAME! ☐

ACT.67

DON'T JUDGE A COVER BY ITS BOOK

Remember when you were a wee child in elementary school and your sexy teacher would show you how to make a book cover for your reading primer?

Remember how you loved it when she leaned over you, her long blonde hair brushing against your forearm... Well, this act enables you to relive the feeling! (But without the tiny, tight feeling in your pants.) This is good and fun and goodfun. It requires a bit of arts and craftiness.

- Take some books out of the library. The daft-er the better. Anything about the Battle of Hastings or Richard Branson is perfect.
- Get some sticky paper that resembles the colour of the book spine you will be copying. I can't go into any further detail.
- Write a new title, making it look as professional as possible, then stick it over the current title.
- Put it back on the shelf.
- Watch for hours as everyone walks by then go home.

Here are some examples of titles you can use:

- *When Animals Attack, Hilarity Ensues*
- *Star Wars 18: The Fucking Begins*
- *How to Start A Pandemic*
- *Richard Branson Shags His Private Plane*

ACT.68

SPOILING THE SPOILER

You're on a holiday. Cyprus. Or Crete. Yes, Crete is better. It's July. No, December. Your boyfriend is reading a mystery novel which he just can't seem to put down. Despite your attempts to lure him into an afternoon sex romp or even banal conversation, he will not be swayed. *'As soon as I'm done, honey. Then we can boink.'*

Do this: the next time he is away from his book (possibly speaking to a bellboy or evacuating his bowels), you must spring into action. And remember, you must work fast.

1. Get the book and read the last chapter. Hurry!

2. Scan it for any telltale clues of revelation. Examples might be:

   • *'And so I came to realize that the murderer is...'*
   • *'The man wasn't in fact my father after all, but my paedophilic mother!'*
   • *'The aliens came towards me and started to probe my...'*

3. Rip out the last chapter and replace it with a Post-it note or something sticky that says: *'If you want to know how it ends, come into the bedroom,'* or, *'Ha, wouldn't you like to know, ya cunt.'* (This, of course, depends on the style of communication you normally use with your partner.)

4. Be prepared to give him the missing pages after certain favours; or if he's being a stubborn twat, just eat the damn thing in front of him.

I DID IT! ☐   I'M LAME! ☐

ACT.69
PAPER TRAIL TALE

Have you ever come across a slip of paper in an old book or magazine and found it miles more fascinating than the stuffy old book you started with? Things like old '*to do*' lists, directions, love letters, pharmaceutical instructions... It all makes you wonder about the person, what they were doing and who they were bumming.

Why not give this gift of voyeuristic wonder to someone else in the future? A '*time capsule*' if you will. And I will. There's something wrong with me.

1. Cut out a piece of paper.

2. Write stuff on it.

3. Hide it somewhere that someone is eventually bound to find it.

4. Go on a six-month cruise to Easter Island.

5. If you haven't forgotten about the slip of paper yet, bash yourself on the head with a *Life on Mars* coffee mug.

Here are some ideas of things to write:

- A tasty confession. Write a note that confesses something really good, like: '*I burned down the house at no. 12 Clancy Street in Reading. I did it because it took my virginity.*'

- Anything Jesus. It helps if you know how to write in ancient Aramaic (as opposed to the modern day hip-hop Aramaic). Write something like, '*I am the modern-day prophet returning to Earth to deliver salvation and buy a delicious Subway sandwich and a Diet Pepsi with a bag of those yummy Sun Chips.*'

- A treasure map. Draw an old map (adding tea stains can help achieve the *'old timey'* part), which mentions some treasure like *'Gold found during the Battle of Trafalgar'*. Make sure the directions lead the reader nowhere, or, if you're an evil sadist, make it a specific place so the recipient spends eighteen hours digging, only to wind up in the lingerie section at H&M.
- Hint at its intrinsic value on ebay. Make it look like someone famous once owned the book. Try writing something like, *'I'm Eddie Izzard. This is a great book!'* in the margins. This may seem a bit subtle, but don't forget, I'm the expert, not you.

Note: This act does not have to be limited to a book. Other possible places to leave intriguing slips of paper are: inside a pillow, a safe, or in a mold of jelly shaped like a child's head. That's it. There are no other possible places.

ACT.70

FAHRENHEIT FOUR-FIFTY-FUN

I love to burn books, almost to the point of self-pleasure. And no, it's not because I'm a pyromaniac (I gave up my membership three years ago). No, I love book-burning because it's so unexpected, particularly in a non-Nazi society. You only ever hear about it when reading articles like *'Signs That Your Teenager May Be a Serial Killer'*. Book-burning usually rates third, after torturing rabbits and cheating at poker.

Try this out one night when you're at a cottage with friends, sitting in front of the hearth, roasting figs and telling traditional Demi Moore stories. As the flames start to dwindle and Tom, the chiropractor-who-picks-his-toes, offers to go outside to get some kindling, stop him and say, *'I got it, buddy.'* Then proceed straight to the bookshelf, pick up the most flammable book you can find (old ones with dusty pages are the best), and casually toss it on the fire. Watch your friends' jaws drop to emit loud, yodelly screams. When they shout, *'What the fuck do you think you're doing?!'*, simply respond with: *'Look, a saddle with eyes!'* Then run out the door.

Books that nobody reads are best, so anything by John Grisham is a good candidate.* Another good choice is the Bible, especially the part about Leviticus. What a snooze fest.

*Correction: I meant books that nobody *interesting* reads.

I DID IT! ☐ I'M LAME! ☐

CHAPTER 09

HUMAN RELATIONSHIPS

FAMILIES,
PARTNERS,
KIDS,
FRIENDS,
DISTANT COUSINS,
NAKED UNCLES,
INBRED PETS...

ACT.71

WHO'S YOUR DADDY?

Let's be honest, kids are coddled to death these days. They expect the world to be filled with candies, cupcakes and enchanted pies that magically make more candies, cupcakes and enchanted pies. Is it any wonder that if one thing goes wrong for these kids (like they get dumped, lose their job or get caught with a busload of coke), they react in an ape-shitty way?

It's time we showed kids disappointment at an early age. For example, if you are playing your niece at Chinese checkers, you must defeat her with no mercy. Let her know that you are an adult, which means you are to be honoured and respected, and that you are fully capable of beating the shit out of her.

If the kid is a bona fide genius and he can already kick your ass at say, golf, then you must find other things at which you can best him. At the very least, remind the kid that you can do things that he can't. *'Hey Billy, I'm going to drive a car right now and then have sex with my girlfriend.'* Done. Eat that you idgit. I said eat... Mmm, enchanted pies.

I DID IT! ☐   I'M LAME! ☐

ACT.72

MARIA VON TRAPPED

Let's say you've got a boyfriend or a wife or a dogfriend who makes you feel trapped and stifled, but you know that for whatever reason (such as legal documents, children, or a very lucrative will), you're not getting out. This can take its toll on your mental health and is also not good for your digestive system. You need to commit a tiny act just in order to stay healthy.

1. Think about your situation. Do you feel trapped? Lonely? Unfulfilled? Are you frustrated that the dog can't speak to you? Be totally honest with yourself.

2. Write it down on a piece of paper (or the bathroom mirror in lipstick or blood).

3. After reading the note, does it make you want to leave the piece of paper lying around the flat? Sure, you wouldn't tell your significant other this fact directly, but if your mind-thoughts should just happen to come out by accident, that's not your fault, right?

4. Do it. Leave a note that says '*I FEEL TRAPPED*' betwixt all the takeaway menus.

There, that's it. You've let it out into the universe. Wheels have been set in motion. You have rebelled against your own chicken shittedness. And if your partner asks you about your '*I feel trapped*' message, you can either talk about it or you can make something up like, '*It's a new West End play with Kevin Spacey. Did you know he likes dogs?*' There, you've done it. Well done.

Note: You can also modify this to reveal a personal pet peeve you have about the person in question, for example by writing a note saying: '*You take too long to shower*'. It's less traumatic, but let's face it, you're not going to do the '*trapped*' one anyway, are you?

I DID IT! ☐   I'M LAME! ☐

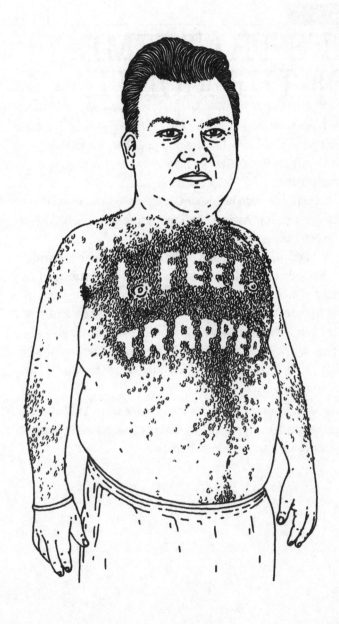

ACT.73

IT'S THAT TIME OF THE MONTH

You know those subscription cards that are always falling out of magazines? If you're like me, you find them a nuisance, useful only for things like taping together to make a pair of summer pants.

But here's an even better idea. Let's say someone has been harassing you for charity donations or tickets to *Wicked* or just plain being an ass pain.

Go to the newsstands and while the vendor is busy staring into his belly-button fold, grab a handful of those subscription cards and take them home. Now fill them in with the name of your harasser and mail them off. In no time, your ex-dentist will be receiving issues of *Sudoku Times*, your councilwoman will be getting *Soldier of Fortune*, and your nosey mother-in-law who snoops around your flat will be reading *Wound Penetrators Monthly* magazine. Victory.

Note: Watch out for paper cuts, they're the worst kind of cut. Especially if, like me, you enjoy soaking your hands in lemon juice after a long day at the fish market.

I DID IT! ☐   I'M LAME! ☐

ACT.74

LOVE ME BLENDER, LOVE ME SWEET

When I was a wee thing (let's say twenty-four), I went through a phase where I was driven to snog inanimate objects. The bedpost, the TV, magazines... nothing was safe from my crazed OCD lips.

If I were to do this now, however, it would be off to the booby hatch for sure. You're not supposed to kiss things. It's just not done. For some arbitrary reason, you're supposed to kiss people. Placing your puckered lips upon another person's spotty skin is fine and dandy – but snogging a refrigerator magnet is verboten. What the effing eff word?!

I have made it my goal in life to take on this kissy-faced double standard – and now you get to benefit from my pain.

1. While having dinner with a friend, gently kiss every morsel of food before you eat it. Try not to break the flow of conversation. *'So, I talked to Georgie* [kiss mash] *today and she thought* [kiss lamb] *we should start to see* [kiss beer twice] *a counsellor because she thinks* [snog plate violently] *I have a problem.'*

2. Try focusing on one food in particular, for example, the green beans. A good way to think about this is to treat it as a pet. *'You're my little sqwoogy woogy aren't you? Aren't you?'* Kiss, kiss, kiss...

3. If you're feeling bolder, step it up and properly romance the objects of your affection. French-kiss a carrot peeler, perhaps. Maybe try feeling up a mobile phone. For some reason, Nokias are really randy.

4. Move past objects and into the realm of non-inanimate objects: your human friends. Start greeting them in different ways. When they go for the cheek kiss, just plant one right between the elbow and the shoulder. Or lick the top of their hand. It's a surefire conversation starter.

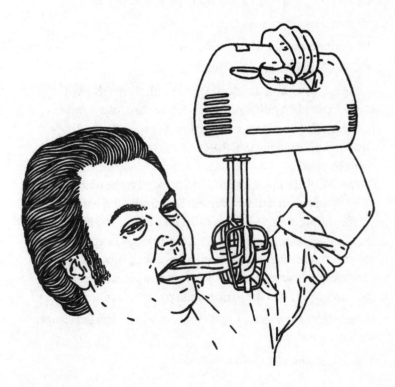

ACT.75

NOBODY 'NO's THE TROUBLE I'VE SEEN

I'm no parent, but I understand that it can be difficult to say no:

'No candy.'

'No cookies before breakfast.'

'No throwing knives at your grandfather.'

And as the child gets older, the 'no's persist:

'No parties while I'm away.'

'No driving in the house.'

'No, No, No, No, No!'

According to some kids, it's all one big... uh, I can't think of the right word.* We all know that children are hard-wired to try things they're not supposed to do. Whether it's smoking cigarettes or throwing tomahawks at crowds below, they're going to try it.

Cut yourself some slack and head them off at the pass. Do all these things in private, by yourself. You're not a hypocrite if you're puffing weed in the towel-jammed closet, you're merely rebelling against your child by rebelling against your own rules so as to counteract his/her eventual rebellion... how was that? I don't know how it all works. So go ahead and watch porn on the internet, eat that deep-fried hand, you're an adult, godammit!

Note: But you don't have to get pregnant with a stranger or sleep with the Royal Navy.

* 'No.' That was the word I forgot.

I DID IT! ☐   I'M LAME! ☐

ACT.76
ELOPE

....

Find someone totally repugnant to your family – whether it be your father's ex-wife, a member of Al Qaeda or a Tory – and run away and get married.

Okay, so this is not a tiny act. But if you do it, it's worth about eight finger points.

I DID IT! ☐   I'M LAME! ☐

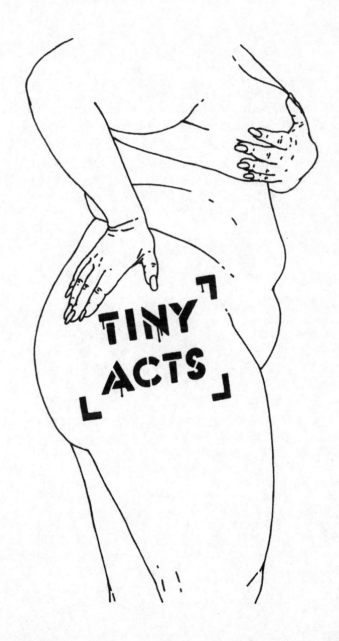

CHAPTER 10

WORK

OFFICES, INTERVIEWS, LUNCH MEETINGS, TEAM-BUILDING EXERCISES, PORNOGRAPHIC SCREENSAVERS...

ACT.77

DRESS ME DOWN, BEFORE YOU GO-GO

Being forced to wear a corporate 'uniform' is just another way that the Man puts his talons into your individuality.

'But oh, what's this? Dress-down Fridays? What a gift! Oh, thank you soooo much for allowing me to express my individuality by taking off my tie! Let me show you my appreciation by licking your stapler.'

This is the perfect opportunity to reveal the innate ridiculousness of Casual Fridays for what they are: a dangling carrot designed to make us feel grateful for just being comfortable.

Imagine your supervisor's delight when, instead of wearing jeans and a T-shirt on Dress-down Friday, you don a pair of jodphurs and a riding crop, or a French Renaissance outfit à la *Dangerous Liaisons*. A bra made out of egg cartons also makes a nice choice.

Let's get realsies. In about ten years, we're all going to be doing office work on Skype in shit-stained pyjamas anyway, so why not hit the ground running.

Suggestions:

- **Sub-casual:** nappy (feel free to use for its intended purpose)
- **Casual:** ass-less hospital gown
- **Super-Casual:** WWI Infantryman outfit

I DID IT! ☐ I'M LAME! ☐

ACT.78

TAKING CREDIT WHERE CREDIT IS DEBIT

When I am lecturing universities about this book*, I get all sorts of questions like, *'Where do you normally part your hair?'* and *'Why do you hang outside my flat staring at my wife through a telescope?'* But that has nothing to do with this particular tiny act.

I feel that I can generalize when I say that people don't appreciate it when others take credit for their stuff. Whether it be a speech or a joke or a moonlanding, if the right person doesn't get credit for it, they get very, very angry. Sort of like when you shove someone right before they're about to take a bite to eat. They react primordially, lashing out without thinking.

Next time you're around someone who receives a compliment, take absolute credit for it... all of it. So if someone lauds your friend on his office attire, say you picked it out. Or if someone tells your colleague she gave a good speech at a conference, say you wrote it. If someone says, *'Wow, it's such a nice day outside,'* reply, *'Thanks for noticing, I'm glad you like it.'*

Chances are the intended complimentee will be upset. Don't worry. You have two options:

1. Say *'I was just kidding. Jeez, it's only a flowered tie. Go ahead and take your compliment, man.'* Or

2. Hold steadfast until everyone leaves, then tell him in private.**

*I mostly speak at *'In My Own Mind'* University.
**But you have to give me credit for reading it here.

I DID IT! ☐   I'M LAME! ☐

ACT.79

AND I JUST CAN'T HIDE IT

Do you ever get put off when some jerko at the office gets so excited about some boring fact that you think about setting fire to yourself? Example: *'Oh my god, I'm going to the dry cleaners today and I can't wait to see if the stain came out of my favourite blouse!'*

This will usually be followed by an overly exuberant story about going to the cleaners, too, complete with snappy verbal exchanges.

People who get hopped up over such mundane things are either trying to convince themselves that life is interesting in all its facets or they are loons who need loads and loads of brain-dead pills.

There are two ways to rebel against such a person:

1. Go negative. This requires a swift counter-offensive, which is aimed at deflating the opponent – I mean co-worker – immediately.

    Co-worker: *'Oh my god, I went and fed these cute little pigeons today and...'*

    You: *'Did you know that pigeons transmit AIDS?'*

    Boom. She's cooked. The conversation will go in an *'Is-this-AIDS-thing-true?'* direction and she won't have time to regroup.
2. Fight fire with mucho fire, i.e. you get even more excited than the eager beaver. Jump on the story like stink on a shitpile to render your colleague impotent. So when some dude mentions his great seats at the football on Sunday...

    You: *'Wait, you had seats, what's that like?'*

    Co-worker: *'Well, they were great, Row 14 and we could see...'*

    You: *'No, sitting, what's it like to sit down? I love sitting but I can never*

do it right, you know, cuz there's a bone in your bum and it hurts...'
Boom. Done. The reaction will be one of resignation or an epiphany
that they are the object of scorn as you ask them about breathing.
Godspeed diffusing these office crazies. They must be stopped, I tell
you, they must be stopped.

ACT.80

DUCKING OUT OF WOIK

When I worked as a paranormal at a law firm, I always announced my departure from the office before I left. *'Bye, see ya tomorrow,'* I'd say, only to be met with, *'Hey Rich, could you come here for a minute?'* There would always be more filing or casework and I would wind up staying an extra hour and would end up late for my date with a very convincing transsexual and I hated it soooo @#$%$@! much.*

This can easily be avoided by pulling a Houdini at the office (see Tiny Act #30). Suckers announce when they're leaving. They are asking for punishment, much like those guys in Opus Dei with the prickly thigh chains (or cilicie for you medieval religious freaks) that keep digging into the skin.

There are several ways to leave the office stealthily. First and foremost, never announce your departure, and never, never, never say goodbye. Once you start doing this, you set a bastard ugly precedent in which you are viewed as that nice woman that everyone can pick on. Secondly, now that you've made this life choice, you will establish an exact opposite precedent.

'Where's Sasquatch?'

'Oh, who knows, I never know where he is'.

Good. Ways to duck out:

- Go for a fag – and then a smoke (hello, I'll be here all week), then just leave.
- Say, *'Hey, I'm going to the shoppes, does anybody want anything?'* Pray they say no, then book it.

....

- Sneak down the stairwell. Be sure to take your shoes.
- Yell something inciting (inciteful) like *'Fire!'* or *'Crocodile on the loose!'* or *'There's a sale on* Star Wars *memorabilia across the street!'* or *'There's a nude geriatric walk-a-thon across the street!'* This is really desperate and can only be used once.
- Make the rounds, visiting with employees who are situated closer and closer to the front door. When you finally reach reception (try not to have a briefcase or a bag which will make you look like you're leaving), pop off to the toilet, and out the window.
- Ask the receptionist, *'What time is it?' '3.15' 'Shit!'* and run out.
- Develop a minor, but obvious skin affliction so that you need to go to the dermatologist on a regular basis. Again the prickly thigh thing might come in handy here.

* Translation: soooo cocksucking much.

NINE TO WHAT?

This act is strictly for those in gainful employment.

1. If you are employed, please skip ahead to step 3.

2. If you are not employed, please put this book down, pick up a newspaper and find a job. Then proceed to step 3.

3. Show up for work, albeit for five seconds, on a non-work day, and announce to everyone on Monday or the day after that you showed up to work on the weekend/holiday. Your co-workers will either admire you or scoff at your blatant arse kissing. This somewhat erratic behaviour will rebel against those who keep normal (i.e. anally tight) working hours.

If you traipse in and out of work, coming and going at random hours, your boss is likely to view you as a devoted employee – even though you show up far less than the schmuck who works every day from ten till six or nine to five or bleepitybling to bloopedybop.

Just imagine the disdain you'll feel when you're presented with a Work Achievement Award, while your co-workers sit there stupefied, smouldering in their cold roast beef with a treacle sponge pudding dripping off the plate. (I don't know why I said that.)

I DID IT! ☐   I'M LAME! ☐

ACT.82

LET'S BE PRANK

I don't know about you Miss Fancy-Pants or Mr GravyThong, but I was pranked quite a bit as a child. So much so that my only defence was to perform pranks upon myself in order to beat others to the punch. Now that I am a responsible adult, flat-renter (with parental support), and owner of thirty-two Café Nero loyalty cards, I feel comfortable enough with myself to bring this practice back.* Here are some things you can do to yourself that will say to the world, *'I'm being fucked with'*:

- Staple your dress or trousers to another item of your clothes. A blouse or a suit jacket will suffice. Make sure that it is visible to others.
- Put large goops of marmalade on your stapler and keyboard mouse. Make sure someone sees you use it so that you can get the full dosage of ridicule and/or sympathy.
- Make a sign on A4 paper and tape it to your back with the message: *'Office Dickhead'*, *'King of the Wankers'* or the ole standby *'Kick The Crap Out of Me'*. Extra points if you wear the sign to an important multi-national meeting.
- Pick up the phone and look shocked, then angrily retort, *'This is outrageous, I repeat, there is no Richard Hertz here… Who's Dick Hertz?'*

The key to all of these is to act oblivious to the prank and make it seem that you have been subjected to this nonsense all of your life. Other people's reactions will speak volumes about their personality and you will then find it easy to compile a list of who to be mean to in the future.

And if you develop a reputation as a prankee, your boss will take pity on you and give you money and then you can tell mum and dad to stop telling you what to do! Whaaaa.

*And with the help of proper anti-anxiety medication.

☐ I DID IT!   ☐ I'M LAME!

ACT.83

WHAT'S ON THE CV?

This is very similar to Tiny Act #48 only it pertains specifically to the CV. How many of us have not put a slight embellishment on this document at one time or another? Huh?

I said Huh???

That four-and-a-half month internship at the Bank of Scotland that is deftly rounded up to six months. That time you went scuba-diving in Aruba which is magically transformed into you being a *'certified scuba instructor'*. The time you yelled at that skinny kid for leaning on your car and screamed, *'Don't you know how much it costs to detail a 1989 Nissan Stanza?!'* that became *'Tutored economics to underprivileged children'*... It's all good, right?

As you can see, this is more of an anarchic twist than trying to put your best foot forward. Slip in a decidedly bogus detail or two to see if the employer is really paying attention. Here are some suggested entries, organized by section:

- **Personal Details:** Put down the most outrageous email name you have for a contact, like daddygonnagetyou69@hotmail.com. Also, write in a good middle name like Spicket or Bucko or Prissy.
- **Work Experience:** It's always good to have active verbs like *'liaise'* or *'spearheaded'*, but in your case *'destroyed'* and *'perverted'* might be even better.
- **Education:** Under a listing of grades, put down *'!!!'* or *'yes'* under one of them.

- **Hobbies and Interest:** It's always entertaining to put down
  Charrrrrrrdsna as a second language. Other things to mention are:
  eats fruit, accepts bribes, farm spotting, and adept at hunting tacos.
  If at any time you are called out for these insertions, either explain
  them away (e.g. *'The !!! grades are based on excitement levels and that's
  the highest'*) or simply pull out the most universal excuse known to
  humans: *'Oh, it's a typo.'*

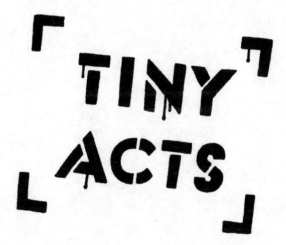

CHAPTER 11

BAD ETIQUETTE

EATING HABITS,
POSTURE,
PERSONAL
GROOMING,
SOCIAL
BEHAVIOUR,
MAINTAINING
THE VERY FABRIC
OF SOCIETY...

ACT.84

FLIPPING THE UNDER-BIRD!

Isn't it annoying having to be cordial to people you hate, loathe, despise, or even love intensely? Don't you wish there was another way? There is.

Step 1. Find someone you hate and talk to them from across a table or desk.

Step 2. Casually lower your hand (either one is preferable) until it is beneath the tabletop.

Step 3. Apply the aforementioned '*under-bird*' *(see illustration 17c).

The trick to this one is not giving it away. Don't 'lean' into your bird, nor should you allow yourself to break out into a shit-eating grin or make an '*I-hate-your-ass*' grimace. It only brings attention to your flicking and also may look as though you are jerking off.

The artistry in this tiny act is to have a normal conversation so that your '*friend*' will walk away smiling, ignorant of the fact that you have just non-verbally told him to '*fuck off*'.

* For some unknown reason, this act does not work in France and in some parts of the Galapagos Islands. I think it has something to do with the magnetic field.

I DID IT! ☐   I'M LAME! ☐

ACT.85
THE FISH-FINGER HANDSHAKE
(AKA: THE LAZY HADDOCK)*

I make terrible first impressions. I hate the idea of someone making instant judgments about me based on my attire, hair, hygiene and footwear... mainly because I'm a failure at all of them. I'd much rather be judged on my deliberately retarded behaviour than on something as innocuous as a handshake.

So the next time you know you are going to be introduced to someone new, try this on for size (and by size, I mean all one-and-a-half inches).

1. Apply a healthy amount of lotion to your hand. I recommend a jigger's full.
2. Relax the hand as if it were a lazy haddock.
3. Extend your hand, but make no effort to grasp or clutch the hand of the introductee.

Observe the reaction. There will an instantaneous recoil of horror, followed by a forced smile and a thinly veiled excuse to leave, like *'Hey, I think my fondue sticks are on fire!'*

'But Rich,' you say. *'Isn't the point to make friends?'*

'Listen', I say. *'Contrary to what you may think, I happen to have loads of friends. I can't really summon them up right now because I need a good lead time. You kind of caught me short notice, but they are around. And by the way, how dare you interrupt my book with a personal question like that? Where do you get off??? Don't answer that.'*

* Does not work with animals (exception: gibbons).

I DID IT! ☐   I'M LAME! ☐

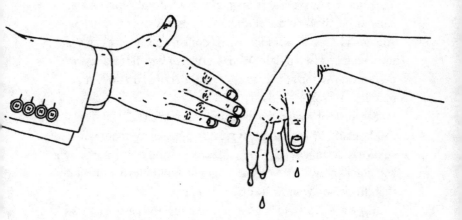

ACT.86

HONK IF YOU LOVE HONKING

Why is it that only gaggles of women at hen parties and people on parade floats wave at strangers? Rebel. Thumb your nose at conventionality – and at thumbs and noses. Wave at someone you don't know. This is most easily done if you are in a car. Wait until you are at a red light. When it turns green, honk and wave at someone as you accelerate. Watch the confusion in your rearview mirror.

For those of you who don't think this is an act of 'rebellion', think again. We have implicit rules in our society about when to be nice to strangers: i.e., never. Just waving and smiling at people you don't know is a tiny act of insurgence and future protection that the person won't kill you at a later date.

If you are a bit bolder, pretend you know the person and walk up to them. *'Evita? Is that you?'* When they vehemently deny your recognition, act really disappointed and walk away on the verge of tears. Another tactic is to move on to another person immediately if you're turned down. *'Evita? Evita? Is that you?'* (This is particularly funny when used on men.)

I DID IT! ☐ I'M LAME! ☐

ACT.87

WHAT I'M 'SAYING' IS 'VERY' IM'PORT'ANT

Often used as material for standups at the Laugh-eteria (I eat most of my jokes there), air quotes are ubiquitous in society. For those of you who don't know what air quotes are because you live in a cave, I'm referring to the act of bobbing the index and second finger of both hands up and down when speaking a word or phrase, in order to designate either false importance or derision.

Here's an example: a group of ladies are in a café. One of them asks, *'Where is Amanda today?'* Another woman responds: *'Oh, she's at her [air quotes] "tennis lesson" [end air quotes].'* The implication is that she's not really having a tennis lesson, she's bonking the tennis pro. Another example would be if you were giving a lecture on pigeons, you may start out by saying, *'[air quotes] "Pigeons" [end air quotes] were invented in 1735.'* This, of course, refers not to the bird itself but to the mechanical version.

My feeling is that people are far too cavalier with air quotes these days. When I was a tyke, we were lucky to use one air quote a year, and that was only on special occasions.

Before this annoying gesticulation becomes the [air quotes] *'norm'* [end air quotes], we must replace it quickly with something else.

Here are some suggestions for alternative [air quotes] *'air quote'* [end air quotes] activities:

- **'The Air Flap'** or **'The Poultry Quote':** Place your hands in each pit and flap your arms like a chicken when using air quotes.

- **'The Whirling Cock':** Stand up and rotate 360 degrees.

- **'The Air-Horn Quote':** Instead of gesticulating, just speak very loudly and succinctly.

- **'The Footnote':** Use your feet instead of your hands.

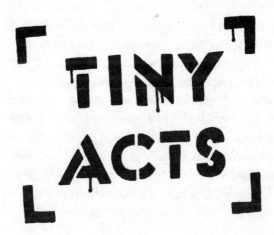

ACT.88

FARTS AND CRAFTS

Science tells us that farting is the body's way of expelling gas that has become trapped in the upper and lower intestine. Other theories tell us that any time a fart is released into the universe a troll gets a blowjob.

Regardless of which farting camp you're in, all agree that backdoor trumpeting in most cultures is considered socially unacceptable. But, did you know...?

- Napoleon would emit popcorn farts in order to inspire his troops before battle. Strangely enough, he forgot to pass gas before the Battle of Waterloo.
- William *'Sugar Tits'* Wallace anally exhaled the word *'freedom'* just before being beheaded.
- After his death, medical records show that JFK's lifeless colon tooted for forty-two minutes straight.*

Historical precedents aside, let's say that you're in the middle of purchasing something at the chemist, say a box of super-plus tampons for your grandpa's poker night. The clerk processes your payment and hands over your change. As you walk away, you casually remark, *'Thank you... Oh, and by the way, I just farted.'*

'But Rich,' you say. *'Unlike you, I cannot shoot the wind beneath my cheeks on command.'* FORGET ABOUT ACTUALLY FARTING. It's funnier if you don't even rectally heave. Not only will the victim be stunned, they will be vainly sniffing the air for flatulence long after you've departed. Besides, it's merely the suggestion of a butt boom – like a bomb threat – that is the real terrorist act.

On the occasion where you are in possession of an actual butt burp, I recommend announcing them as they occur. Some ideal phrases to use are:

- *'Bombs away!'*
- *'Hello, ladies!'*
- *'Nana Mouskouri!'*
- *'Burritos on the house!'*

*Curiously, Winston Churchill never made a poo noise during the entirety of WWII.

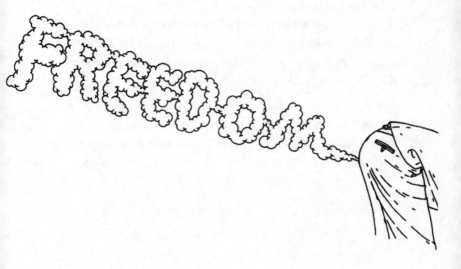

ACT.89

SIR WAVES-A-LOT

Since the publication of this book (actually, it hasn't been published yet. Wait, what? I'm lying? Get my lawyer on the phone!), many people have stopped me on the street and asked me to rate my favourite meats and cheeses. They've also asked, *'Rich, how do you handle getting trapped in a boring conversation?'* As I start to answer, I become distracted by something over the fan's shoulder; I look off into the distance and begin to wave furiously. I then apologize to the person and tell him that I have just spotted an old and dear friend (in reality, a cloud formation) and walk off, smiling with glee. And that's precisely how I get out of a potentially boring discussion about the merits of Gouda with some idiot who was stupid enough to buy this book.*

Try this even if you're with a person who is fascinating. It is endlessly amusing, and almost always works. And on the rare occasion that a cumulo-nimbus cloud waves back at you, you will have just made a major scientific discovery.

Note: If the person follows you, you're fucked, and must pretend you are chasing after your imaginary friend.

* I meant the wonderful man whom I love dearly and for whom I personally signed four books.

I DID IT! ☐   I'M LAME! ☐

ACT.90

BANGERS AND FASH... ION

Everyone likes to stick out to varying degrees. I, personally, like to look like a piece of tree bark. What better way to rebel against the norm than by making a tiny act of fashion?

Here are some thoughts:

- Wear two different shoes. This is always good because it makes you look insane, so if people start throwing rocks at you, there is a good chance that at least one of your shoes has a decent tread on it and you'll be able to hop away quickly.
- Shave off half your beard.* I did this once and went to a party, and half the people didn't even notice. Of course, it may have been because I had also shaved off half my exposed pubes.
- Wear underpants over your trousers. This *Clockwork Orange* look will turn heads, and not just because of the rancid stink.
- Mix plaid with stripes. Looking like a lesbian banker is always a great option.
- Don a vest with lights. Wearing lights is great for the holidays, as well as for those late-night spelunking piss-ups.
- Wear white patent leather shoes in winter. If this isn't off-putting enough, put pictures of serial killers on the toes.

These are but a few suggestions for rebellious fashion items. The main thing to consider is to follow your instincts. As Oscar Wilde once said, *'Fashion feeds the depths of your soul until it digs deep beneath your blood and bones – .'* Wait, I think that was Stephen King.

* If you are a woman and don't have a beard, you should be ecstatic.

FLIPPING OFF EVERYTHING IN SIGHT

Don't confuse this with flipping the under-bird (Tiny Act #84). In this scenario, you shouldn't really care who you're two-finger saluting. Say you're walking down the street, you can give the finger to a shoe store, that blade of grass sticking out of the pavement, that parked Saab near your nan's Prius. It doesn't matter. It helps if you have a witness, otherwise you may just be viewed as a shy ASBO (doesn't that sound like a film, *The Shy ASBO* from Columbia Pictures?). Flicking a V to dogs and babies is particularly special. Who knows, if enough people do this, it could evolve into being a popular greeting. It could be one of those gestures that has about fifty meanings, like the word *'aloha'* or *'shag'*.

Note: Make sure you don't give a two-fingered salute to some random yobbo who might have a knife. This tiny act requires a certain amount of social discretion.

I DID IT! ☐   I'M LAME! ☐

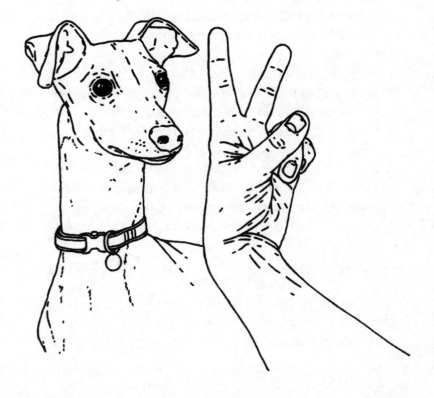

ACT.92

I'M HOOKED ON ONE-UPPERS

Ever been around a guy who always has to one-up you? No matter what story you tell, he has to follow it up with something like, *'That's nothing, when I was in the Israeli Army I captured a platoon of beef-tipped steak.'*

This is especially tiresome if you're in the middle of trying to impress someone else. It's kind of like a verbal form of *'Cock Blocking'* (*'Cunt Shunt'* for the ladies).

There's got to be a way to stop these annoying people. Here's how:

1. Put the pressure on. Before he launches into his diatribe, say something to the effect of, *'Are you trying to one-up me with a better story? Okay, but this had better be good.'*
2. Interrupt as often as possible. Interject throughout with comments like, *'Get out!'*, *'You're full of shite'* or *'I hate you'*.
3. After the one-upper is done, make up another story that one-ups his even more – *'Are you aware that I invented deep dish pizza?'* and *'Did you know that I'm related to Good King Wenceslas?'* Most likely, he will not be prepared for this and will retreat.

Let's try this out: your hilarious story of getting lost in Morocco is one-upped by Tom's tale of being robbed by two street urchins in Kuala Lumpur. But then you casually mention that you were sold as a sex slave in a Vietnamese enema camp and were raped by a TV, winning the day and the attention of all within earshot.

I DID IT! ☐   I'M LAME! ☐

ACT.93

PUBLIC DISPLAYS OF ERECTION

Most people hate PDAs (public displays of affection). They also are not fond PDBs (public displays of blowies), PDWs (public displays of wanking) and PDSATDTMITB (public displays of sex acts too disgusting to mention in this book).

Some places are more acceptable for PDAs than others. While a pair exchanging neck nuzzles in a quiet corner at the pub wouldn't afford more than a casual glance, a couple violently snogging at a cousin's funeral could possibly cause an uproar – unless it was part of the ceremony.

Whether you're a single guy who hasn't been laid since Blair was cool, or you regularly partake in four-ways with the Bulgarian Navy, this tiny act will suit rebels of every sexual ability. All you need is a willing partner and a box of eight-ply condoms.*

Here are some ideas for places to take part in inappropriate PDAs:

· During couples therapy.

· When playing doubles in tennis (during a point).

· At a business lunch.

· During divorce proceedings.

· At a kid's birthday party.

* **Note:** You can also do this alone, in which case you no longer need the condoms.

I DID IT! ☐   I'M LAME! ☐

ACT.94

CLOSE TO OOH

Personal body space is an issue with most people. Sure, we need to get used to the nudges and pokes associated with large concerts, rush-hour tube rides and general twenty-first-century urban lifestyle, but not when there's no one around.

Next time you're in an empty café and there's a lone man sitting in the corner (angry feminists take note: I say man because if you are a man and the person sitting alone is a woman then you simply risk looking like a perv*), sit uncomfortably close to him. Scrunch your chair closer and closer, reach over him for the sugar... Start reading a book and lean it against his side of the table. It will be mind-bendingly unnerving for the man. If the guy says something, just yell: *'Do you mind?'*

But keep on – this is more than a tiny act. This is an act of public service. You're making people aware of space. It's the final frontier, you know. Try it in different locations – it also works well in lifts, cinemas, empty fields, swimming pools and with groundskeepers at empty football stadiums. Oh, and with dental surgeons when they're mid-extraction.

*However, if you are a pervert, then please disregard this note.

I DID IT! ☐   I'M LAME! ☐

ACT.95

PLEASE RE-LEASH ME

If you're ever lucky enough to have a baby, there's a lot of cool stuff you can do with her/him/it/shit.* Take, for instance, the generally held belief that you should constantly check on the baby during the early months of its non-pregnancy (post-inside-the-guts life). That's where the leash comes in. Growing in popularity for young children of walking age, why not apply the same *'leash'* philosophy for babies?

Find a suitable dog collar that fits your baby. When friends come over, simply put it around shit's neck and see if anyone notices.

Try hiding the lead so you can get someone to say, *'Isn't shit a little young to have a necklace?'* To which you respond: *'Oh, that's not a necklace* [produce the lead], *it's a leash. Ooh, I think shit's getting away!'*

Watch the hilarity ensue as your friends struggle to determine whether to yank the baby from your hands or call social services. Ho ho.

I can hear the letters now; I can also see the verbal complaints: *'Rich, this is easy for you to recommend, you don't even have any children.'* Well, I've never been to Mars but that doesn't mean I can't say anything about Martians. I need to work on that.

Another thing you can do with the leash is put it on yourself and train your dog to use it. You need to do this totally straight-faced as the dog drags you from doggy dish to couch to lawn to park bench to opposing dog's anus to maggot-infested rubbish bin near the dilapidated school to couch to lawn to dish.

Note: If you don't own a dog or baby, borrow one.

*Hereinafter referred to as 'shit' so as not to worry about pronouns.

ACT.96

YOU STUPID BITCH

Public arguments are intoxicating. I'll never forget the endless fights I heard sleeping next to an alley in Queen's Park. After a while, it became white noise, like a waterfall that sent me off to Sleepytime Village. Give the gift that keeps on giving – start a public argument... with a dog.

This can be difficult. The trick is to work your way up to it. Start by questioning the headlines to your newspaper. *'TOTTENHAM HOTSPUR BEAT ARSENAL?... WONDERDRUG INDUCES MENOPAUSE?'*

'Okay,' the passers-by are thinking, *'he's just mad at the headlines.'* But there's more.

Lay the paper down on a bench and shake your head disapprovingly, as you shout at it in more personal detail: *'You slut, sitting there in black and white like some high-heeled slag. I saw you out with an OK! magazine last night! Where's your travel section?! Did you give it away to some homeless squirrel again?!'*

Try this with several inanimate objects throughout the day until you're ready to graduate to an animal.

Next, try your dog. Make sure it resembles the spat a couple might have:

'You are going to die of cancer if you eat one more poop, do you understand me?'

'Rex, I am not putting up with your book clubs any more.'

If done properly, you will not only be feared but also entirely avoided by the rest of the world.

I DID IT! ☐   I'M LAME! ☐

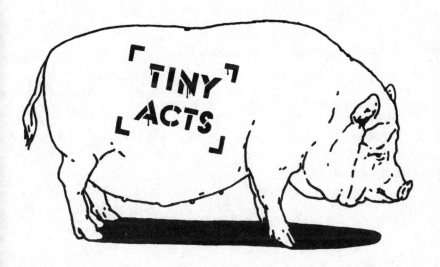

CHAPTER 12

OTHER

READING
THIS BOOK

ACT.97

READING THIS BOOK

Welcome comrade. You've taken an important step on the road to rebellion... The Road to the Tiny Acts (a.k.a.: Tiny Acts Avenue) – or where Tottenham Court Road meets Leyton Way. Just as the biggest small village begins with a single large city, this book will help you grow into a fully formed eunuch capable of taking on the challenges of modern-day life.

Carry this book with you wherever you go. Stick it in a purse or a naval rucksack made of kelp. It is sturdily designed for the long-haul, with the knowledge that it may take you, dear reader, a great deal of time to accomplish these acts. I expect to see dog-eared, bent and freshly raped copies all over the streets and villages of the UK, Europe and with any luck, Belgium.

Everyone will approach the book differently. I knew a man from Djakarta, not really, who completed all the acts in just two days. He's dead now. Other people will never finish. To you, I say, *'Fuck off'*. But everyone's tiny activist journey will be different. That's the beauty of the Tiny Acts philosophy. It's as profound as [insert something profound here].

It won't be easy. But if you are vigilant and follow the book without a prodigious amount of paper cuts, you will thrive. I have faith in you. Now go out there and Stick it to the Man!

With Lust and Plenty of Gas,

Rich Fulcher

Note: If you didn't buy this book and downloaded it illegally on your super-charged Kindle, all of the above words are negated and will change into evil spells, which will make your breasts concave and turn any food you eat into stabby icicles.